15 MINUTE
FRENCH
LEARN IN JUST 12 WEEKS

WITHDRAWN

Caroline Lemoine

DK | Penguin Random House

Senior Editors Angeles Gavira, Christine Stroyan
Project Art Editor Vanessa Marr
Jacket Design Development Manager Sophia MTT
Jacket Designer Juhi Sheth
Pre-Producer David Almond
Senior Producer Ana Vallarino
Associate Publisher Liz Wheeler
Publishing Director Jonathan Metcalf

**Language content for Dorling Kindersley by g-and-w publishing.
Produced for Dorling Kindersley by Schermuly Design Co.**

First American Edition, 2005
This revised edition published in the United States in 2018
by DK Publishing, 1450 Broadway, Suite 801,
New York, NY 10018, USA

18 19 20 21 22   10 9 8 7 6 5 4 3 2
003–305459–Jan/2018

Published in Great Britain by Dorling Kindersley Limited.

A catalog record for this book is available from the
Library of Congress.
ISBN 978-1-4654-6294-7

DK books are available at special discounts when
purchased in bulk for sales promotions, premiums, fund-
raising, or educational use. For details, contact DK
Publishing Special Markets, 1450 Broadway, Suite 801,
New York, NY 10018, USA or SpecialSales@dk.com

Printed in China

A WORLD OF IDEAS:
SEE ALL THERE IS TO KNOW

www.dk.com

CONTENTS

How to use this book | 4

WEEK 1
INTRODUCTIONS
Hello | 8
Relatives | 10
My family | 12
To be and to have | 14
Review and repeat | 16

WEEK 2
EATING AND DRINKING
In the café | 18
In the restaurant | 20
To want | 22
Dishes | 24
Review and repeat | 26

WEEK 3
MAKING ARRANGEMENTS
Days and months | 28
Time and numbers | 30
Appointments | 32
On the telephone | 34
Review and repeat | 36

WEEK 4
TRAVEL
At the ticket office | 38
To go and to take | 40
Taxi, bus, and metro | 42
On the road | 44
Review and repeat | 46

WEEK 5
GETTING AROUND

Around town	48
Finding your way	50
Sightseeing	52
At the airport	54
Review and repeat	56

WEEK 6
ACCOMMODATION

Booking a room	58
In the hotel	60
At the campground	62
Descriptions	64
Review and repeat	66

WEEK 7
SHOPPING

Shops	68
At the market	70
At the supermarket	72
Clothes and shoes	74
Review and repeat	76

WEEK 8
WORK AND STUDY

Jobs	78
The office	80
Academic world	82
In business	84
Review and repeat	86

WEEK 9
HEALTH

At the pharmacy	88
The body	90
At the doctor	92
At the hospital	94
Review and repeat	96

WEEK 10
AT HOME

At home	98
In the house	100
The backyard	102
Pets	104
Review and repeat	106

WEEK 11
SERVICES

Post office and bank	108
Services	110
To come	112
Police and crime	114
Review and repeat	116

WEEK 12
LEISURE AND SOCIALIZING

Leisure time	118
Sport and hobbies	120
Socializing	122
Review and repeat	124
Reinforce and progress	126

MENU GUIDE	128
ENGLISH–FRENCH DICTIONARY	132
FRENCH–ENGLISH DICTIONARY	146
Acknowledgments	160

How to use this book

The main part of the book is devoted to 12 themed chapters, broken down into five 15-minute daily lessons, the last of which is a revision lesson. So, in just 12 weeks you will have completed the course. A concluding reference section contains a menu guide and English-to-French and French-to-English dictionaries.

18   WEEK 2

Warm up (1 minute)

Count to ten (pp.10–11).

Remind yourself how to say "hello" and "goodbye." (pp.8–9)

Ask "Do you have a baguette?" (pp.14–15)

AU CAFÉ
In the café

In a typical French café you can either s counter, which is cheaper, or have wait a table. Tipping is the norm if you're service, but a few coins will be enough. usually served, although you can often and croissants in the mornings.

Words to remember (5 minutes)

Look at the words below and say them out loud a few times. Cover the French with the flap and try to remember the French for each item. Practice the words on the picture also.

le café crème *luh kafay krem*	coffee with frothy milk
le grand café *luh groñ kafay*	large black coffee
le thé *luh tay*	black tea
le thé au lait *luh tay oh lay*	tea with milk

le café *luh cafeh* small black

le sucre *luh sookruh* sugar

Cultural tip A standard coffee is small and black. You need to ask if you want it any other way. If you like milk in your tea, you'll need to specify cold milk (**lait froid/** lay frwah), otherwise you are likely to get a jug of hot mi

In conversation (4 minutes)

Bonjour. Je voudrais un café au lait, s'il vous plaît.
bonjoor. juh voodray uñ kafay oh lay, seel voo play

C'est tout madame?
say too ma-dam
Is that all, madam?

Vous avez *voo zavay c*
Do you hav

Warm up

Each day starts with a warm up that encourages you to recall vocabulary or phrases you have learned previously. To the right of the heading bar you will see how long you need to spend on each exercise.

Instructions

Each exercise is numbered and introduced by instructions that explain what to do. In some cases additional information is given about the language point being covered.

Cultural/Conversational tip

These panels provide additional insights into life in France and language usage.

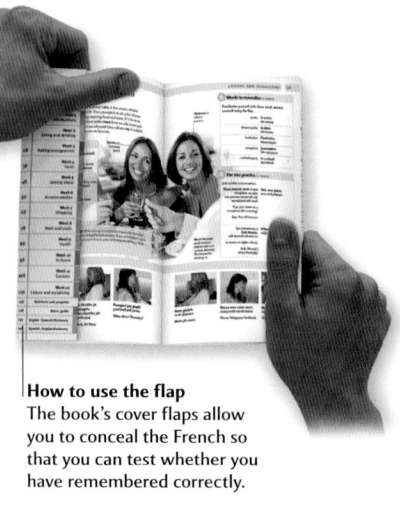

How to use the flap

The book's cover flaps allow you to conceal the French so that you can test whether you have remembered correctly.

Revision pages

A recap of selected elements of previous lessons helps to reinforce your knowledge.

16   WEEK 3   MAKING ARRAN

Réponses
Answers (Cover with flap)

RÉVISEZ ET RÉPÉTEZ
Review and repeat

1 Suros

❶ seize
sez
❷ trente-neuf
tront-nerf
❸ cinquante trois
sankont-trwah
❹ quatre-vingt
*dix-neuf
katruh-vañ deesnerf*
❺ quarante-et-un
karont ay-uñ

1 Sums (4 minutes)

Say the answers to these sums out loud in French. Then check that you have remembered correctly.

❶ 10 + 6 = ?
❷ 14 + 25 = ?
❸ 66 – 13 = ?
❹ 40 + 34 = ?
❺ 90 + 9 = ?
❻ 46 – 5 = ?

3 Telephones (3 minutes)

What are the numbered items in French?

cell phone ❶

headphones ❷

answering ❸ machine

SIM card ❹

telephone ❺

2 I want...

❶ voulez
voolay
❷ veut
veh
❸ voulons
vooloñ
❹ veux
veh
❺ veux
veh
❻ veut
veh

2 I want... (3 minutes)

Fill the blanks with the correct form of *vouloir.*

❶ Vous ____ un café?
❷ Elle ____ aller en vacances.
❸ Nous ____ une table pour trois.
❹ Tu ____ que bière?
❺ Je ____ une nouvelle voiture.
❻ Il ____ des bonbons.

4 When? (2 minutes)

What do these sentences mean?

❶ J'ai rendez-vous lundi vingt mai.
❷ Mon anniversaire est en septembre.
❸ Je reviens dimanche.
❹ Ils ne travaillent pas en août.

5 Time (3 minutes)

Say these times in French.

Useful phrases
Selected phrases relevant to the topic help you speak and understand.

4 Useful phrases (5 minutes)

Learn these phrases. Read the English under the pictures and say the phrase in French as shown on the right. Then conceal the French with the cover flap and test yourself.

le pain
luh pañ
bread

le café au lait
luh kafay oh lay
large coffee with milk

Je voudrais un grand café, s'il vous plaît.
juh voodray uñ groñ kafay, seel voo play

I'd like a large black coffee, please.

C'est tout?
say too

Is that all?

Je prends un croissant.
juh pron uñ krossoñ

I'll have a croissant.

C'est combien?
say koñbyañ

How much is that?

Oui, bien sûr.
wee, byañ syur

Yes, certainly.

Alors deux croissants. C'est combien?
alor duh krossoñ. say koñbyañ

Two croissants, then. How much is that?

Quatre euros, s'il vous plait.
katruh uroh, seel voo play

Four euros, please.

Text styles
Distinctive text styles differentiate French and English, and the pronunciation guide.

In conversation
Illustrated dialogues reflecting how vocabulary and phrases are used in everyday situations appear throughout the book.

Say it
In these exercises you are asked to apply what you have learned using different vocabulary.

6 Say it (2 minutes)

Do you go near the train station?

The fruit market, please.

When's the next bus to Calais?

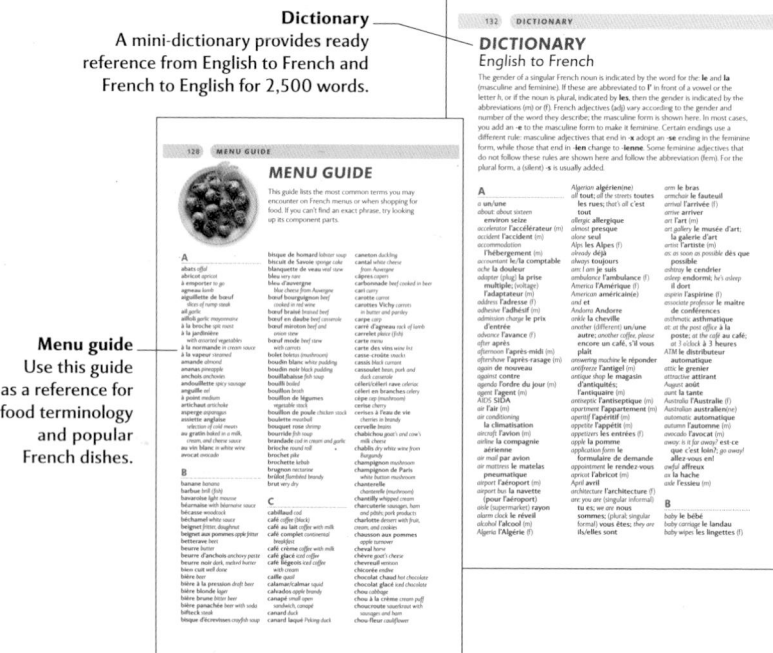

Dictionary
A mini-dictionary provides ready reference from English to French and French to English for 2,500 words.

Menu guide
Use this guide as a reference for food terminology and popular French dishes.

Pronunciation guide

Many French sounds will already be familiar to you, but a few require special attention. Take note of how these letters are pronounced:

r   a French **r** is pronounced in the back of the throat, producing a sound a little like gargling

j   a French **j** is soft like the sound in the middle of *pleasure* (as opposed to the hard English *j* as in *major*)

n   **n** is pronounced nasally when in the combination **on**, **an** or **in**. Imagine saying *huh* through your nose. The nasal **n** is shown in the pronunciation with this symbol: **ñ**

ch   ch in French is equivalent to sh in English, as in *ship*

er/ez these endings are pronounced ay as in *play*

Pay attention also to these vowel sounds as they may vary from English:

     i   as the English *keep*
     au   as the English *over*
     eu   as the English *fur*
     oi   as the English *wag*

After each French word or phrase you will find a pronunciation transcription. Read this, bearing in mind the tips above, and you will achieve a comprehensible result. But remember that the transcription can only ever be an approximation and that there is no real substitute for listening to and mimicking native speakers.

How to use the audio app

All the numbered exercises in each lesson, apart from the Warm-ups at the beginning and the Say it exercises at the end, have recorded audio, available via a free app. The app also includes a function to record yourself and listen to yourself alongside native speakers.

To start using the audio with the book, first download the **DK 15 Minute Language Course** app on your smart-phone or tablet from the App Store or Google Play. Open the app and scan the QR code on the back of this book to add it to your Library. As soon as the QR code is recognized, the audio will download.

There are two ways in which you can use the audio. The first is to read through your 15-minute lessons using the book only, and then go back and work with the audio and the book together, repeating the text in the gaps provided and then recording yourself. Or you can combine the book and the audio right from the beginning, pausing the app to read the instructions on the page as you need to. Try to say the words aloud, and practice enunciating properly. Detailed instructions on how to use the app are available from the menu bar in the app.

Remember that repetition is vital to language learning. The more often you listen to a conversation or repeat an oral exercise, the more the language will sink in.

Menu, Help/How to Use, Your Library

1 Getting started
The list of weeks will open when the audio has been downloaded. From here you can tap into each week's lessons.

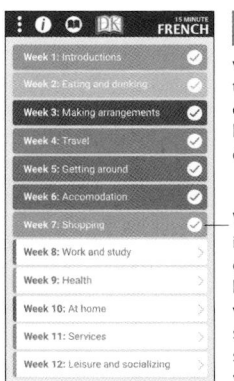

When all the lessons in a week have been completed, the week button will be filled with color and show a check mark, so you can track your progress.

2 Lessons week by week
Each numbered exercise in a lesson is listed in the app as it appears in the book. Tap on an exercise to start.

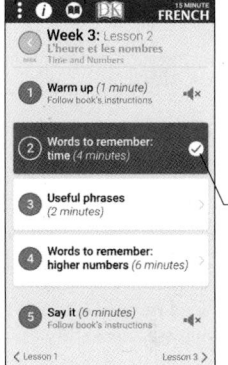

A check mark indicates when an exercise has been completed.

3 Audio for exercises
Tap the play button to hear instructions, then the exercise. You can pause the audio at any point, and return to it.

You can tap any part of the exercise to play the audio from that point.

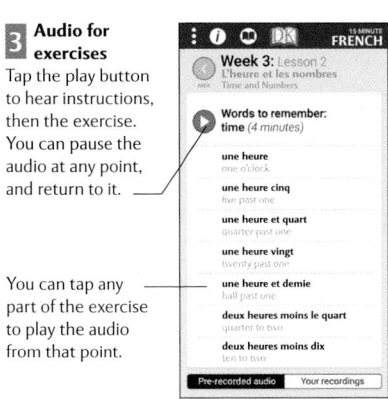

4 Record yourself
When you are in the *Your recordings* screen, you can record yourself reading the words or participating in the conversations with native speakers, then listen back (and rerecord if desired).

Add recording

Play recording

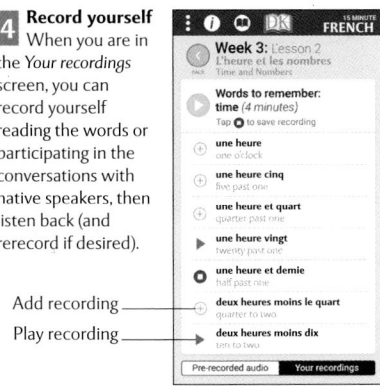

① Warm up (1 minute)

The Warm Up panel appears at the beginning of each topic. Use it to reinforce what you have already learned and to prepare yourself for moving ahead with the new subject.

BONJOUR
Hello

In France it is part of the culture to greet family and friends with kisses on the cheek. The number of kisses varies from two to four. For example, it is usually three kisses in the south but two in Brittany. In more formal situations, a handshake is part of the normal greeting.

② Words to remember (2 minutes)

Salut!
saloo
Hi!

Look at these polite expressions and say them aloud. Cover the text on the left with the cover flap and try to remember the French for each item. Check your answers.

Bonjour. *boñjoor*	Hello.
Bonsoir/bonne nuit. *boñswar/bon nwee*	Good evening/ good night.
Je m'appelle Jean. *juh mapell joñ*	My name is Jean.
Enchanté (men)/ **Enchantée** (women). *oñshontay*	Pleased to meet you.

Cultural tip The French tend to greet people with **monsieur** (*sir*), **madame** (*madam*, for older women), or **mademoiselle** (*miss*, for younger women) much more than most English speakers would.

③ In conversation: formal (3 minutes)

Bonjour. Je m'appelle Céline Legrand.
boñjoor. juh mapell seleen luhgroñ

Hello. My name is Céline Legrand.

Bonjour madame. Monsieur Rossi, enchanté.
boñjoor ma-dam. musyuh rossee, oñshontay

Hello (madam). Mr. Rossi, pleased to meet you.

Enchantée.
oñshontay

Pleased to meet you.

4 Put into practice (3 minutes)

Join in this conversation. Read the French beside the pictures on the left and then follow the instructions to make your reply. Then test yourself by concealing the answers on the right with the cover flap.

Bonjour monsieur.
boñjoor musyuh.

Hello, sir.

Say: Hello, mademoiselle.

Bonjour mademoiselle.
boñjoor mad-mwazel

Je m'appelle Martine.
juh mapell marteen.

My name is Martine.

Say: Pleased to meet you.

Enchanté.
oñshontay

5 Useful phrases (3 minutes)

Familiarize yourself with these phrases. Read them aloud several times and try to memorize them. Conceal the French with the cover flap and test yourself.

Goodbye.	**Au revoir.** *ovwar*
See you soon.	**A bientôt.** *ah byañtoe*
See you tomorrow.	**A demain.** *ah dumañ*
Thank you (very much).	**Merci (beaucoup).** *mairsee (bohkoo)*

6 In conversation: informal (3 minutes)

Alors, à demain?
alor, ah dumañ

So, see you tomorrow?

Oui, au revoir.
wee, ovwar

Yes, goodbye.

Au revoir. A bientôt.
ovwar. ah byañtoe

Goodbye. See you soon.

Warm up (1 minute)

Say "hello" and "goodbye" in French. (pp.8–9)

Now say "My name is…" (pp.8–9)

Say "sir" and "madam." (pp.8–9)

LES RELATIONS
Relatives

In French, the same word is used for relationships by marriage: **beau-père** means both father-in-law and step-father, and **belle-fille** means daughter-in-law and stepdaughter. The French for *the* is **le** or **la**, and *a* is **un** or **une**, depending on whether the word is masculine or feminine (see below).

Match and repeat (5 minutes)

Look at the people in this scene and match their numbers with the vocabulary list at the side. Read the French words aloud. Then cover the list with the flap and test yourself.

❶ **le grand-père**
luh groñpair

❷ **le frère**
luh frair

❸ **la sœur**
lah sur

❹ **le père**
luh pair

❺ **la mère**
lah mair

❻ **la grand-mère**
lah groñmair

❼ **le fils**
luh fees

❽ **la fille**
lah feeyuh

❶ grandfather

brother ❷

❸ sister

❹ father

❺ mother

grandmother ❻   ❼ son   ❽ daughter

Conversational tip In French, things as well as people are masculine (m) or feminine (f). For example, *wine* is masculine: (**le vin**) but *car* is feminine: (**la voiture**). For the plural **les** is used for both masculine and feminine. In this book (m) or (f) indicates the gender after a plural.

3 Words to remember: relatives (4 minutes)

le mari
luh maree
husband

la femme
lah fam
wife

Look at these words and say them aloud. Conceal the text on the right with the cover flap and try to remember the French. Check your answers. Then practice the phrases below.

Nous sommes mariés.
Noo som mareeay
We are married.

sister-in-law/ stepsister	**la belle-sœur** *lah bell sur*
brother-in-law/ stepbrother	**le beau-frère** *luh boe frair*
half-sister	**la demi-sœur** *lah dumee sur*
half-brother	**le demi-frère** *luh dumee frair*
children	**les enfants** (m) *lay zoñfoñ*
I have four children.	**J'ai quatre enfants.** *jay katruh oñfoñ*
I have two stepdaughters.	**J'ai deux belles-filles.** *jay duh bell feeyuh*

4 Words to remember: numbers (3 minutes)

Memorize these words. Now cover the French and test yourself.

Be careful with the pronunciation of **deux** and **trois**. When you say them in front of a word that starts with a vowel, you need to say an extra "z" sound–for example, **deux enfants** (*two children*) is pronounced duh zoñfoñ, and **trois éclairs** (*three eclairs*), trwah zayclair. This is also true of other words.

one	**un/une** *uñ* (m)/*oon* (f)
two	**deux** *duh*
three	**trois** *trwah*
four	**quatre** *katruh*
five	**cinq** *sank*
six	**six** *sees*
seven	**sept** *set*
eight	**huit** *weet*
nine	**neuf** *nurf*
ten	**dix** *dees*

5 Say it (2 minutes)

I have five sons.

I have three sisters and a brother.

I have two stepsons.

① Warm up (1 minute)

Say the French for as many members of the family as you can. (pp.10-11)

Say "I have two sons." (pp.10-11)

MA FAMILLE
My family

The French have two ways of saying *you*: **vous** for people you meet or don't know very well and **tu** for family and friends. Similarly, there are different words for *your*. The words for *my* and *your* also change depending on whether they relate to masculine, feminine, or plural nouns.

② Words to remember (5 minutes)

Say these words out loud a few times. Cover the French with the flap and try to remember the French word for each item.

mon *moñ*	my (with masculine)
ma *mah*	my (with feminine)
mes *may*	my (with plural)
ton *toñ*	your (informal, with masculine)
ta *tah*	your (informal, with feminine)
tes *tay*	your (informal, with plural)
votre *votruh*	your (formal, with masculine or feminine)
vos *voe*	your (formal, with plural)

Voici mes parents.
vwasee may paroñ
These are my parents.

③ In conversation (4 minutes)

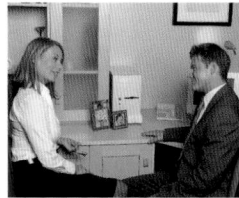

Vous avez des enfants?
voo zavay day zoñfoñ

Do you have any children?

Oui, j'ai deux filles.
wee, jay duh feeyuh

Yes, I have two daughters.

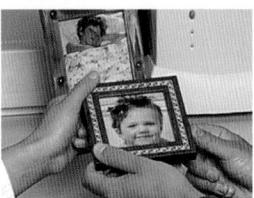

Voici mes filles.
Et vous?
vwasee may feeyuh.
ay voo

These are my daughters. And you?

Conversational tip The French usually ask a question by simply raising the pitch of the voice at the end of a statement—for example, **Vous voulez un café?** (*Do you want a coffee?*). You could also ask the same question by inverting the verb and subject: **Voulez-vous un café?**. Or you can put **Est-ce que** in front of the sentence: **Est-ce que vous voulez un café?**

4 Useful phrases (3 minutes)

Read these phrases aloud several times and try to memorize them. Conceal the French with the cover flap and test yourself.

Do you have any brothers? (formal) — **Vous avez des frères?**
voo zavay day frair

Do you have any brothers? (informal) — **Tu as des frères?**
tew ah day frair

This is my husband. — **Voici mon mari.**
vwasee moñ maree

That's my wife. — **C'est ma femme.**
say mah fam

Is that your sister? (formal) — **C'est votre sœur?**
say votruh sur

Is that your sister? (informal) — **C'est ta sœur?**
say tah sur

5 Say it (2 minutes)

J'ai un beau-fils.
jay uñ boe fees

I have a stepson.

Do you have any brothers and sisters? (formal)

Do you have any children? (informal)

I have two sisters.

This is my wife.

1 Warm up (1 minute)

Say "See you soon."
(pp.8-9)

Say "I am married"
(pp.10-11) and
"I have a daughter."
(pp.12-13)

ETRE ET AVOIR
To be and to have

There are some essential verbs for you to learn in this course. You can use these to construct a large variety of useful phrases. The first two are **être** (*to be*) and **avoir** (*to have*). Learn them carefully, since French verbs change more than English ones according to the pronoun (I, you, etc.) used.

2 Etre: to be (5 minutes)

Familiarize yourself with the different forms of être (*to be*). Use the cover flaps to test yourself and, when you are confident, practice the sample sentences below.

je suis *juh swee*	I am
tu es *tew ay*	you are (informal singular)
il/elle est *eel/el ay*	he/she is
nous sommes *noo som*	we are
vous êtes *voo zet*	you are (formal singular or plural)
ils/elles sont *eel/el soñ*	they are

Je suis anglaise.
juh swee zonglayz
I'm English.

Je suis fatigué(e). *juh swee fatigay*	I'm tired.

Elle est heureuse? *el ay tururz*	Is she happy?

Nous sommes français. *noo som froñsay*	We're French.

3 Avoir: to have (5 minutes)

Il a deux baguettes.
eel ah duh baget
He has two baguettes.

Practice **avoir** (*to have*) and the sample sentences, then test yourself.

I have	**j'ai** / *jay*
you have (informal singular)	**tu as** / *tew ah*
he/she has	**il/elle a** / *eel/el ah*
we have	**nous avons** / *noo zavoñ*
you have (formal singular or plural)	**vous avez** / *voo zavay*
they have	**ils/elles ont** / *eel/el zoñ*

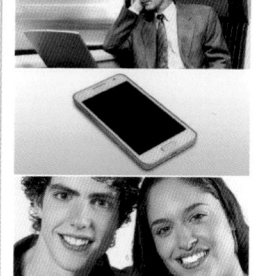

He has a meeting.	**Il a un rendez-vous.** / *eel ah uñ roñday-voo*
Do you have a cell phone?	**Vous avez un portable?** / *voo zavay uñ portabluh*
How many brothers and sisters do you have?	**Vous avez combien de frères et sœurs?** / *voo zavay koñbyañ duh frair ay sur*

4 Negatives (4 minutes)

To make a sentence negative in French, put **ne** in front of the verb and **pas** just after: **nous ne sommes pas anglais** (*we are not English*). If **ne** is followed by a vowel, it becomes **n'**: **je n'ai pas d'enfants** (*I don't have any children*). But many French people drop the **ne** when they're talking, so you'll just hear **nous sommes pas** (*we aren't*), **j'ai pas** (*I haven't*), and so on. Read these sentences aloud, then cover the French with the flap and test yourself.

le vélo
luh vayloe
bicycle

Je n'ai pas de voiture.
juh nay pas duh vwatyur
I don't have a car.

He's not married.	**Il n'est pas marié.** / *eel nay pah mariyay*
I am not sure.	**Je ne suis pas sûr(e).** / *juh nuh swee pah syur*
We don't have any children.	**Nous n'avons pas d'enfants.** / *noo navoñ pah doñfoñ*

Réponses
Answers (Cover with flap)

RÉVISEZ ET RÉPÉTEZ
Review and repeat

1 How many?

1 trois
trwah

2 neuf
nurf

3 quatre
katruh

4 deux
duh

5 huit
weet

6 dix
dees

7 cinq
sank

8 sept
set

9 six
sees

1 How many? (2 minutes)

Cover the answers with the flap. Then say these French numbers out loud. Check that you have remembered the French correctly.

3 **2** 9 **3** 4
1
2 **4** **5** 8 10 **6**
5 7 6
7 **9**
8

2 Hello

1 Bonjour. Je m'appelle... [your name].
boñjoor. juh mapell...

2 Enchanté(e).
oñshontay

3 Oui, et j'ai deux fils. Et vous?
wee, ay jay duh fees. ay voo

4 Au revoir. A demain.
ovwar. ah dumañ

2 Hello (4 minutes)

You meet someone in a formal situation. Join in the conversation, replying in French according to the English prompts.

Bonjour. Je m'appelle Nicole.
1 Answer the greeting and give your name.

Voici mon mari, Henri.
2 Say "Pleased to meet you."

Vous êtes marié(e)?
3 Say "Yes, and I have two sons. And you?"

Nous avons trois filles.
4 Say "Goodbye. See you tomorrow."

3 To have or be (5 minutes)

Fill in the blanks with the correct form of **avoir**
(*to have*) or **être** (*to be*). Check that you have
remembered the French correctly.

❶ Je _____ anglaise.

❷ Nous _____ quatre enfants.

❸ Elle _____ une belle-fille.

❹ Vous _____ rendez-vous?

❺ Il n' _____ pas fatigué.

❻ Je n' _____ pas de portable.

❼ Tu n' _____ pas sûr?

❽ Nous _____ français.

3 To have or be

❶ suis
swee

❷ avons
avoñ

❸ a
ah

❹ avez
avay

❺ est
ay

❻ ai
ay

❼ es
ay

❽ sommes
som

4 Family (4 minutes)

Say the French for each of the numbered family
members. Check that you have remembered the
French correctly.

grandfather ❶
brother ❷
❸ sister
❹ father
❺ mother
grandmother ❻
❼ son
❽ daughter

4 Family

❶ le grand-père
luh groñpair

❷ le frère
luh frair

❸ la sœur
lah sur

❹ le père
luh pair

❺ la mère
lah mair

❻ la grand-mère
lah groñmair

❼ le fils
luh fees

❽ la fille
lah feeyuh

AU CAFÉ
In the café

Warm up (1 minute)

Count to ten (pp.10-11).

Remind yourself how to say "hello" and "goodbye." (pp.8-9)

Ask "Do you have a baguette?" (pp.14-15)

In a typical French café you can either sit at the counter, which is cheaper, or have waiter service at a table. Tipping is the norm if you're happy with the service, but a few coins will be enough. Food is not usually served, although you can often get bread and croissants in the mornings.

Words to remember (5 minutes)

Look at the words below and say them out loud a few times. Cover the French with the flap and try to remember the French for each item. Practice the words on the picture also.

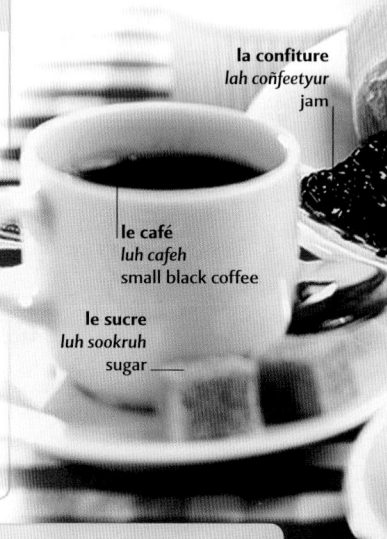

la confiture
lah coñfeetyur
jam

le café
luh cafeh
small black coffee

le sucre
luh sookruh
sugar

le café crème *luh kafay krem*	coffee with frothy milk
le grand café *luh groñ kafay*	large black coffee
le thé *luh tay*	black tea
le thé au lait *luh tay oh lay*	tea with milk

Cultural tip A standard coffee is small and black. You'll need to ask if you want it any other way. If you like milk in your tea, you'll need to specify cold milk (**lait froid/** lay frwah), otherwise you are likely to get a jug of hot milk.

In conversation (4 minutes)

Bonjour. Je voudrais un café au lait, s'il vous plaît.
bonjoor. juh voodray uñ kafay oh lay, seel voo play

Hello. I would like coffee with milk, please.

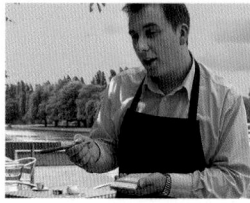

C'est tout madame?
say too ma-dam

Is that all, madam?

Vous avez des croissants?
voo zavay day krossoñ

Do you have any croissants?

(4) Useful phrases (5 minutes)

Learn these phrases. Read the English under the pictures and say the phrase in French as shown on the right. Then conceal the French with the cover flap and test yourself.

le pain
luh pañ
bread

I'd like a large black coffee, please.

Je voudrais un grand café, s'il vous plaît.
juh voodray uñ groñ kafay, seel voo play

Is that all?

C'est tout?
say too

I'll have a croissant.

Je prends un croissant.
juh pron uñ krossoñ

le café au lait
luh kafay oh lay
large coffee with milk

How much is that?

C'est combien?
say koñbyañ

Oui, bien sûr.
wee, byañ syur

Yes, certainly.

Alors deux croissants. C'est combien?
alor duh krossoñ. say koñbyañ

Two croissants, then. How much is that?

Quatre euros, s'il vous plaît.
katruh uroh, seel voo play

Four euros, please.

Warm up (1 minute)

Say "I'd like."
(pp.18-19)

Say "I don't have a
brother." (pp.14-15)

Ask "Do you have any
croissants?" (pp.18-19)

AU RESTAURANT
In the restaurant

There is a variety of different types of eating places
in France. In a **café** you can find a few snacks. A
brasserie is a traditional restaurant; the service is
fast and there's usually no need to make reservations.
In the more formal gastronomic restaurants, it is
necessary to book and to dress up.

Words to remember (3 minutes)

Memorize these words. Conceal
the French with the cover flap
and test yourself.

cup **7**

saucer **8**

5 spoon

6 knife

fork **4**

la carte *lah kart*	menu
la carte des vins *lah kart day vañ*	wine list
les entrées (f) *lay zontray*	appetizers
les plats (m) *lay plah*	main courses
les desserts (m) *lay dessair*	desserts
le déjeuner *luh dayjunay*	lunch
le dîner *luh deenay*	dinner
le petit-déjeuner *luh puhtee dayjunay*	breakfast

In conversation (4 minutes)

**Bonjour. Je voudrais une
table pour quatre.**
*boñjoor. juh voodray oon
tabluh poor katruh*

Hello. I would like a table
for four.

**Vous avez une
réservation?**
voo zavay oon raysairvasyoñ

Do you have a reservation?

Oui, au nom de Smith.
wee, oh noñ duh Smith

Yes, in the name of Smith.

4 Match and repeat (5 minutes)

Look at the numbered items in this table setting and match them with the French words on the right. Read the French words aloud. Now, conceal the French with the cover flap and test yourself.

glass ❶

❷ napkin

plate ❸

❶ **le verre**
luh vair

❷ **la serviette**
lah sairvyet

❸ **l'assiette** (f)
lasyet

❹ **la fourchette**
lah forshet

❺ **la cuillère**
lah kweeyair

❻ **le couteau**
luh kootoe

❼ **la tasse**
lah tass

❽ **la soucoupe**
lah sookoop

5 Useful phrases (2 minutes)

Learn these phrases and then test yourself using the cover flap to conceal the French.

What do you have for dessert?	**Qu'est ce que vous avez comme dessert?** *keskuh voo zavay kom dessair*
The check, please.	**L'addition, s'il vous plaît.** *ladeesyoñ, seel voo play*

D'accord. Quelle table préférez vous?
dakor. kel tabluh prayfayray voo

Fine. Which table would you like?

Près de la fenêtre, s'il vous plaît.
pray duh lah fenetruh, seel voo play

Near the window, please.

Mais bien sûr. Suivez-moi.
may byañ syur. sweevay mwah

Of course. Follow me.

Warm up (1 minute)

What are "breakfast", "lunch", and "dinner" in French? (pp.20-1)

Say "I", "you" (informal), "he", "she", "we", "you" (plural/formal), "they" (masculine), "they" (feminine). (pp.14-15)

VOULOIR
To want

In this section, you will learn the present tense of a verb that is essential to everyday conversation– **vouloir** (to want)–as well as a useful polite form, **je voudrais** (I would like). Remember to use this form when requesting something because **je veux** (I want) may sound too strong.

 Vouloir: to want (6 minutes)

Say the different forms of **vouloir** (to want) aloud. Use the cover flaps to test yourself and, when you are confident, practice the sample sentences below.

je veux *juh vuh*	I want
tu veux *tew vuh*	you want (informal)
il/elle veut *eel/el vuh*	he/she wants
nous voulons *noo vooloñ*	we want
vous voulez *voo voolay*	you want (formal/plural)
ils/elles veulent *eel/el verl*	they want

Tu veux du vin? *tew vuh dew vañ*	Do you want some wine?
Elle veut une nouvelle voiture. *el vuh oon noovel vwatyur*	She wants a new car.
Nous voulons aller en vacances. *noo vooloñ zallay oñ vakons*	We want to go on holiday.

Je veux des bonbons.
juh vuh day boñ-boñ
I want some candy.

Conversational tip To say *some*, **de** (*of*) combines with **le**, **la**, or **les** to produce **du** for the masculine, **de la** for the feminine, or **des** for the plural, as in **du café**, **de la confiture**, and **des citrons** (*lemons*). If the sentence is negative, use only **de**, as in **Il n'y a pas de café**. In the same way, **à** (*to*) combines with **le**, **la**, or **les** to produce **au** for the masculine, **à la** for the feminine, and **aux** for the plural.

③ Polite requests (4 minutes)

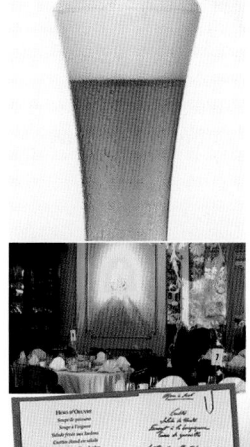

There is a form of **je veux** (*I want*) used for polite requests: **je voudrais.** Practice the sentences below and then test yourself.

I'd like a beer, please.	**Je voudrais une bière, s'il vous plaît.**
	juh voodray oon biyair, seel voo play

I'd like a table for tonight.	**Je voudrais une table pour ce soir.**
	juh voodray oon tabluh poor suh swar

I'd like the menu.	**Je voudrais la carte.**
	juh voodray lah kart

④ Put into practice (4 minutes)

Join in this conversation. Read the French beside the pictures on the left and then follow the English prompts to make your reply in French. Test yourself by concealing the answers with the cover flap.

Bonsoir, madame. Vous avez une réservation?	**Non, mais je voudrais une table pour trois, s'il vous plaît.**
boñswar, ma-dam. Voo zavay oon raysairvasyoñ	*noñ, may juh voodray oon tabluh poor trwah, seel voo play*

Good evening, madam. Do you have a reservation?

Say: No, but I would like a table for three, please.

Quelle table préférez vous?	**Près de la fenêtre, s'il vous plaît.**
kel tabluh prayfayray voo	*pray duh lah fenetruh, seel voo play*

Which table would you like?

Say: Near the window, please.

LES PLATS
Dishes

Say "I'm tired" and "I'm not sure." (pp.14-15)

Ask "Do you have croissants?" (pp.18-19)

Say "I'd like a white coffee." (pp.18-19)

France is famous for its cuisine and the quality of its best restaurants. It also offers a wide variety of regional dishes. Plenty of garlic and butter are a feature of many typical dishes. Although traditionally French cuisine is meat-based, many restaurants now offer a vegetarian menu.

Cultural tip You will usually have the choice of eating a set **menu** or ordering **à la carte**. With a set menu, salad is often a starter and you usually have to choose between dessert or cheese.

2 **Match and repeat** (4 minutes)

Look at the numbered items and match them to the French words in the panel on the left. Test yourself using the cover flap.

❶ les légumes (m)
lay laygoom

❷ le fruit
luh froo-wee

❸ le fromage
luh fromarj

❹ les noix (f)
lay nwah

❺ la soupe
lah soop

❻ la volaille
lah vol-eye

❼ le poisson
luh pwassoñ

❽ les pâtes (f)
lay pat

❾ les fruits de mer (m)
lay froo-wee duh mair

❿ la viande
lah vee-ond

fruit ❷

vegetables ❶

cheese ❸

❺ soup

poultry ❻

❽ pasta

❾ seafood

3 **Words to remember: cooking methods** (3 minutes)

Familiarize yourself with these words and then test yourself.

fried	**frit(e)**	*free(t)*
grilled	**grillé(e)**	*greeyay*
roasted	**rôti(e)**	*rotee*
boiled	**bouilli(e)**	*booyee*
steamed	**à la vapeur**	*ah lah vapur*
rare	**saignant(e)**	*say-nyoñ(t)*

Je voudrais mon steak bien cuit.
juh voodray moñ stayk byañ kwee
I'd like my steak well done.

6 **Say it** (2 minutes)

What is **cassoulet**?

I'm allergic to seafood.

I'd like a beer.

nuts ❹

fish ❼

❿ meat

4 **Words to remember: drinks** (3 minutes)

Familiarize yourself with these words.

water	**l'eau (f)**	*loe*
fizzy water	**l'eau gazeuse (f)**	*loe gazuz*
still water	**l'eau plate (f)**	*loe plat*
wine	**le vin**	*luh vañ*
beer	**la bière**	*lah biyair*
fruit juice	**le jus de fruits**	*luh joo duh froo-wee*

5 **Useful phrases** (2 minutes)

Learn these phrases and then test yourself.

I'm a vegetarian.	**Je suis végétarien.**	*juh swee vejitah-ryañ*
I'm allergic to nuts.	**Je suis allergique aux noix.**	*juh swee zalurzheek oh nwah*
What are "escargots"?	**Qu'est que c'est les "escargots"?**	*keskuh say lay zeskargoh*

Réponses
Answers (Cover with flap)

RÉVISEZ ET RÉPÉTEZ
Review and repeat

1 At the table

❶ les noix
lay nwah

❷ les fruits de mer
*lay froo-wee
duh mair*

❸ la viande
lah vee-ond

❹ le sucre
luh sookruh

❺ le verre
luh vair

1 At the table (4 minutes)

Name the numbered items.

❶ nuts

sugar ❹

seafood ❷

meat ❸

glass ❺

2 This is my...

❶ C'est mon mari.
say moñ maree

❷ Voici ma fille.
vwasee mah feeyuh

**❸ Ma table est
non-fumeur.**
*mah tabluh ay
noñ-foomur*

**❹ Mes enfants sont
fatigués.**
*may zoñfoñ
soñ fatigay*

2 This is my... (4 minutes)

Say these phrases in French.
Use **mon**, **ma**, or **mes**.

❶ This is my husband.

❷ Here is my daughter.

❸ My table is nonsmoking.

❹ My children are tired.

3 I'd like...

❶ Je voudrais un café.
juh voodray uñ kafay

**❷ Je voudrais de
la confiture.**
*juh voodray duh
lah coñfeetyur*

❸ Je voudrais du pain.
juh voodray doo pañ

**❹ Je voudrais un café
au lait.**
*juh voodray uñ kafay
oh lay*

3 I'd like... (3 minutes)

Say you'd like the following:

bread ❸

jam ❷

❶ black coffee

large coffee ❹
with milk

6 pasta

knife **7**

8 cheese

beer **10**

9 napkin

Réponses
Answers (Cover with flap)

1 At the table

6 les pâtes
lay pat

7 le couteau
luh kootoe

8 le fromage
luh fromarj

9 la serviette
lah sairvyet

10 la bière
lah biyair

4 Restaurant (4 minutes)

You arrive at a restaurant. Join in the conversation, replying in French according to the English prompts.

Bonjour madame, monsieur.
1 Ask for a table for six.

Fumeur ou non-fumeur?
2 Say: nonsmoking.

Suivez-moi, s'il vous plaît.
3 Ask for the menu.

Et vous voulez la carte des vins?
4 Say: No. Sparkling water, please.

Voilà.
5 Say: I don't have a glass.

4 Restaurant

1 Bonjour. Je voudrais une table pour six.
boñjoor. juh voodray oon tabluh por sees

2 Non-fumeur.
noñ-foomur

3 La carte, s'il vous plaît.
lah kart, seel voo play

4 Non. De l'eau gazeuse, s'il vous plaît.
noñ. duh loe gazuz, seel voo play

5 Je n'ai pas de verre.
juh nay pah duh vair

LES JOURS ET LES MOIS
Days and months

In French, the *days of the week* (**les jours de semaine**) and *months* (**les mois**) are not capitalized. The months have names similar to the English ones. You use **en** with months: **en avril** (*in April*), but not with days.

2 **Words to remember: days** (5 minutes)

Familiarize yourself with these words and test yourself using the cover flap.

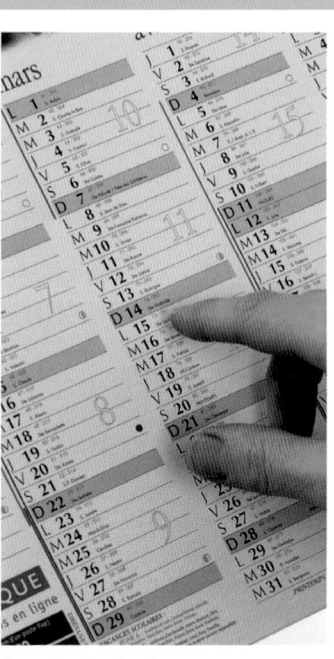

lundi *luñdee*	Monday
mardi *mardee*	Tuesday
mercredi *mairkrudee*	Wednesday
jeudi *jurdee*	Thursday
vendredi *voñdrudee*	Friday
samedi *samdee*	Saturday
dimanche *deemonsh*	Sunday
aujourd'hui *oh-joordwee*	today
demain *dumañ*	tomorrow
hier *eeyair*	yesterday

Demain, c'est lundi.
dumañ, say luñdee
Tomorrow is Monday.

3 **Useful phrases: days** (2 minutes)

Learn these phrases and then test yourself using the cover flap.

La réunion n'est pas mardi. *lah rayoonyoñ nay pah mardee*	The meeting isn't on Tuesday.
Je travaille le dimanche. *juh trav-eye luh deemonsh*	I work on Sundays.

4 Words to remember: months (5 minutes)

Familiarize yourself with these words and test yourself using the cover flap.

Notre anniversaire de mariage est en juillet.
notruh aneevairsair duh mareeaj ay toñ jweeyay
Our wedding anniversary is in July.

Noël est en décembre.
nowel ay toñ daysombruh
Christmas is in December.

January	**janvier**	*joñvyay*
February	**février**	*fevreeyay*
March	**mars**	*mars*
April	**avril**	*avreel*
May	**mai**	*may*
June	**juin**	*jwañ*
July	**juillet**	*jweeyay*
August	**août**	*oot*
September	**septembre**	*septombruh*
October	**octobre**	*oktobruh*
November	**novembre**	*novombruh*
December	**décembre**	*daysombruh*
month	**le mois**	*luh mwah*
year	**l'an** (m)	*loñ*

5 Useful phrases: months (2 minutes)

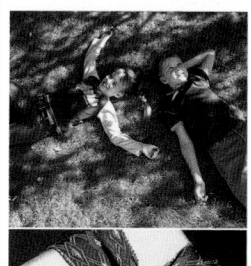

Learn these phrases and then test yourself using the cover flap.

My children are on vacation in August.	**Mes enfants sont en vacances en août.** *may zoñfoñ soñ toñ vakons oñ oot*
My birthday is in June.	**Mon anniversaire est en juin.** *moñ naneevairsair ay toñ jwañ*

1 Warm up (1 minute)

Count in French from
1 to 10. (pp.10-11)

Say "I have a reservation."
(pp.20-1)

Say "The meeting is on
Wednesday." (pp.28-9)

L'HEURE ET LES NOMBRES
Time and numbers

The 12-hour clock is used in everyday speech, while the
24-hour clock is employed in bus stations, airports, etc.
Where the minutes are first in English (*ten to five*),
in French the hour is first: **dix heures moins cinq**
(*ten minus five*).

2 Words to remember: time (4 minutes)

Memorize how to tell the time in French.

une heure *oon ur*	one o'clock
une heure cinq *oon ur sank*	five after one
une heure et quart *oon ur ay kar*	quarter after one
une heure vingt *oon ur vañ*	one-twenty
une heure et demie *oon ur ay dumee*	one-thirty
deux heures moins le quart *duh zur mwañ luh kar*	quarter to two
deux heures moins dix *duh zur mwañ dees*	ten to two

3 Useful phrases (2 minutes)

Learn these phrases and then test yourself using
the cover flap.

Quelle heure est-il? *kel ur ay teel*	What time is it?

A quelle heure voulez-vous le petit déjeuner? *ah kel ur voolay voo luh puhtee dayjunay*	What time do you want breakfast?

J'ai une réservation pour douze heures. *jay oon raysairvasyoñ poor dooz ur*	I have a reservation for twelve o'clock.

4 Words to remember: higher numbers (6 minutes)

In French when you say 21, 31, etc. you say: **vingt-et-un**, **trente-et-un**, and so on. After that, just put the numbers together without et: **vingt-deux** (22), **quarante-cinq** (45).

70 is **soixante-dix** (sixty-ten), 75 is **soixante-quinze** (sixty-fifteen), and so on. **Quatre-vingt** (80) means four-twenties, and 90 is **quatre-vingt-dix** (four-twenties-ten). So 82 is **quatre-vingt-deux** and 97 is **quatre-vingt-dix-sept**.

Ça fait quatre-vingt-cinq euros.
sah fay katruh-vañ-sank uroh
That's eighty-five euros.

eleven	**onze**	*onz*
twelve	**douze**	*dooz*
thirteen	**treize**	*trez*
fourteen	**quatorze**	*katorz*
fifteen	**quinze**	*kanz*
sixteen	**seize**	*sez*
seventeen	**dix-sept**	*deeset*
eighteen	**dix-huit**	*deezweet*
nineteen	**dix-neuf**	*deeznurf*
twenty	**vingt**	*vañ*
thirty	**trente**	*tront*
forty	**quarante**	*karont*
fifty	**cinquante**	*sankont*
sixty	**soixante**	*swasont*
seventy	**soixante-dix**	*swasont-dees*
eighty	**quatre-vingt**	*katruh-vañ*
ninety	**quatre-vingt-dix**	*katruh-vañ-dees*
one hundred	**cent**	*soñ*
three hundred	**trois cents**	*trwah soñ*
one thousand	**mil**	*meel*
ten thousand	**dix mille**	*dee meel*
two hundred thousand	**deux cent mille**	*duh soñ meel*
one million	**un million**	*oon meel-yoñ*

5 Say it (2 minutes)

twenty-five

sixty-eight

eighty-four

ninety-one

five to ten.

eleven-thirty.

What time is lunch?

LES RENDEZ-VOUS
Appointments

1 Warm up (1 minute)

Say the days of the week. (pp.28-9)

Say "It's three o'clock." (pp.30-1)

What's the French for "today", "tomorrow", and "yesterday"? (pp.28-9)

Business in France is generally conducted more formally than in the United States; always address your business contacts as **vous**. The French tend to leave the office for the lunch hour, often having a sit-down meal in a restaurant or, less commonly, at home.

Bienvenue.
byañvenoo
Welcome.

la poignée de main
lah pwanyay duh mañ
handshake

2 Useful phrases (5 minutes)

Learn these phrases and then test yourself.

Prenons rendez-vous pour demain. *prunoñ ronday-voo poor dumañ*	Let's meet tomorrow.
Avec qui? *avek kee*	With whom?
Quand êtes-vous libre? *koñ et-voo leebruh*	When are you free?
Je suis désolé(e), je suis occupé(e). *juh swee dayzolay, juh swee zokupay*	I'm sorry, I'm busy.
Pourquoi pas jeudi? *poorkwah pah jurdee*	How about Thursday?
C'est bon pour moi. *say boh poor mwah*	That's good for me.

3 In conversation (4 minutes)

Bonjour. J'ai rendez-vous.
boñjoor. jay ronday-voo

Hello. I have an appointment.

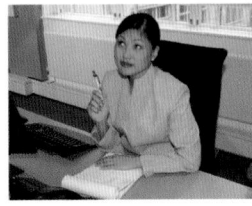

Avec qui?
avek kee

With whom?

Avec Monsieur Le Blanc.
avek musyuh luh bloñ

With Mr. Le Blanc.

4 Put into practice (5 minutes)

Join in this conversation. Read the French beside the pictures on the left and then follow the instructions to make your reply. Then test yourself by concealing the answers on the right with the cover flap.

Prenons rendez-vous pour jeudi.
prunoñ ronday-voo poor jurdee

Let's meet on Thursday.

Say: Sorry, I'm busy.

Je suis désolé, je suis occupé.
juh swee dayzolay, juh swee zokupay

Quand êtes-vous libre?
koñ et-voo leebruh

When are you free?

Say: Tuesday afternoon.

Mardi après-midi.
mardee apray meedee

C'est bon pour moi.
say boñ poor mwa

That's good for me.

Ask: What time?

A quelle heure?
ah kel ur

A quatre heures, si c'est bon pour vous.
ah katruh ur see say boñ poor voo

At four o'clock, if that's good for you.

Say: It's good for me.

C'est bon pour moi.
say boñ poor mwah

Très bien. A quelle heure?
tray byañ. ah kel ur

Okay. What time?

A trois heures, mais je suis un peu en retard.
ah trwah zur, may juh swee uñ puh oñ retar

At three o'clock, but I'm a little late.

Ne vous inquiétez pas. Asseyez-vous, je vous en prie.
nuh voo zañkyetay pah. assayay voo, juh voo zoñ pree

Don't worry. Sit down, please.

1 Warm up (1 minute)

Say "I'm sorry." (pp.32-3)

What is the French for "I'd like an appointment"? (pp.32-3)

How do you say "with whom?" in French? (pp.32-3)

AU TÉLÉPHONE
On the telephone

The emergency number for police, ambulance, or fire services is 112. To make direct international calls, dial 00 followed by the country code, area code (omit the initial 0), and the number. The country code for France is 33.

2 Match and repeat (4 minutes)

Match the numbered items to the French in the panel on the left and test yourself.

1 le chargeur
luh sharjur

2 le téléphone
luh telayfon

3 le répondeur
luh raypoñdur

4 les écouteurs (m)
lay zaykootur

5 le portable
luh portabluh

6 la carte SIM
lah kart seem

telephone **2**

charger **1**

headphones **4**

5 mobile

3 In conversation (4 minutes)

Allô. Pauline Du Bois à l'appareil.
aloh. pawleen doo bwah ah lap-paray

Hello. Pauline du Bois speaking.

Bonjour. Je voudrais parler à Rachid Djamal.
boñjoor. juh voodray parlay ah rasheed jahmal

Hello. I'd like to speak to Rachid Djamal.

C'est de la part de qui?
say duh lah par duh kee

Who's speaking?

SIM card ❻

Je voudrais acheter une carte SIM.
juh voodray ashetay oon kart seem
I'd like to buy a SIM card.

❸ answering machine

I'd like to speak to Mr. Hachart.

Can I leave a message for Emma?

4 **Useful phrases** (4 minutes)

Practice these phrases. Then test yourself using the cover flap.

I'd like the number for Michel.

Je voudrais le numéro de Michel.
juh voodray luh noomairoe duh meeshell

I'd like to speak to Françoise Martin.

Je voudrais parler à Françoise Martin.
juh voodray parlay ah franswahz martañ

Can I leave a message?

Je peux laisser un message?
juh puh laysay uñ mesarj

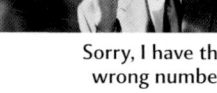

Sorry, I have the wrong number.

Désolé(e), je me suis trompé(e) de numéro.
dayzolay, juh muh swee trompay duh noomairoe

Jean Leblanc de l'imprimerie Laporte.
joñ luhbloñ duh lahpreemuree laport

Jean Leblanc of Laporte Printers.

Désolée. La ligne est occupée.
dayzolay. lah leenyuh et okupay

I'm sorry. The line is busy.

Il peut me rappeller, s'il vous plaît?
eel puh muh raplay, seel voo play

Can he call me back, please?

Réponses
Answers (Cover with flap)

RÉVISEZ ET RÉPÉTEZ
Review and repeat

1 Sums

❶ **seize**
sez

❷ **trente-neuf**
tront-nurf

❸ **cinquante-trois**
sankont-trwah

❹ **soixante-quatorze**
swasont-katorz

❺ **quatre-vingt dix-neuf**
katruh-vañ deeznuf

❻ **quarante-et-un**
karont-ay-uñ

1 Sums (4 minutes)

Say the answers to these sums out loud in French. Then check that you have remembered correctly.

❶ 10 + 6 = ?
❷ 14 + 25 = ?
❸ 66 − 13 = ?
❹ 40 + 34 = ?
❺ 90 + 9 = ?
❻ 46 − 5 = ?

3 Telephones (3 minutes)

What are the numbered items in French?

cell phone ❶

headphones ❺

2 I want...

❶ **voulez**
voolay

❷ **veut**
vuh

❸ **voulons**
vooloñ

❹ **veux**
vuh

❺ **veux**
vuh

❻ **veut**
vuh

2 I want... (3 minutes)

Fill the blanks with the correct form of **vouloir**.

❶ Vous ____ un café?

❷ Elle ____ aller en vacances.

❸ Nous ____ une table pour trois.

❹ Tu ____ une bière?

❺ Je ____ une nouvelle voiture.

❻ Il ____ des bonbons.

answering **②**
machine

SIM card **③**

telephone **④**

Réponses
Answers (Cover with flap)

3 Telephones

❶ le portable
luh portabluh

❷ le répondeur
luh raypoñdur

❸ la carte SIM
lah kart seem

❹ le téléphone
luh telayfon

❺ les écouteurs
lay zaykootur

---

4 When? (2 minutes)

What do these sentences mean?

❶ J'ai rendez-vous lundi vingt mai.

❷ Mon anniversaire est en septembre.

❸ Je reviens dimanche.

❹ Ils ne travaillent pas en août.

4 When?

❶ I have a meeting on Monday, May 20th.

❷ My birthday is in September.

❸ I come back on Sunday.

❹ They don't work in August.

---

5 Time (3 minutes)

Say these times in French.

❶ ❷ ❸ ❹ ❺ ❻

5 Time

❶ une heure
oon ur

❷ une heure cinq
oon ur sank

❸ une heure vingt
oon ur vañ

❹ une heure et demie
oon ur ay dumee

❺ une heure et quart
oon ur ay kar

❻ deux heures moins dix
duh zur mwañ dees

1 Warm up (1 minute)

Count to 100 in tens.
(pp.10-11, pp.30-1)

Ask "At what time?"
(pp.30-1)

Say "Half-past one."
(pp.30-1)

AU GUICHET
At the ticket office

In France, before getting on the train, you must *validate*
(**composter**) your ticket by stamping it. Special orange
machines are installed in every train station for this
purpose. Fines are handed out to those who forget to
validate their tickets. Most trains have both first- and
second-class seats.

2 Words to remember (3 minutes)

Learn these words and then test yourself.

la gare *lah gar*	station
le train *luh trañ*	train
la voiture *lah vwatyur*	car
le billet *luh beeyay*	ticket
aller-simple *allay-sañpluh*	one-way
aller-retour *allay-rutoor*	round-trip
première classe *prumyair klas*	first class
en seconde *oñ sugond*	second class

le passager
luh pasahjay
passenger

le quai
luh kay
platform

La gare est pleine de monde.
lah gar ay plen duh moñd
The station is crowded.

3 In conversation (4 minutes)

**Deux billets pour
Bordeaux s'il vous plaît.**
*duh beeyay poor bordoe
seel voo play*

Two tickets for Bordeaux,
please.

Aller-retour?
allay rutoor

Round-trip?

**Oui. Je dois réserver
des places?**
*wee. juh dwah rayzurvay
day plas*

Yes. Do I need to
reserve seats?

4 Useful phrases (5 minutes)

Learn these phrases and then test yourself using the cover flap.

How much is a ticket to Lille?	**C'est combien un billet pour Lille?** *say koñbyañ uñ beeyay poor leel*
Do you accept credit cards?	**Vous acceptez les cartes de crédit?** *voo zakseptay lay kart duh kredee*
Do I have to change trains?	**Je dois changer?** *juh dwah shonjay*
Which platform does the train leave from?	**Le train part de quel quai?** *luh trañ par duh kel kay*
Are there discounts?	**Vous faites des réductions?** *voo fet day raydooksyoñ*
What time does the train for Paris leave?	**A quelle heure part le train pour Paris?** *ah kel ur par luh trañ poor paree*

Le train pour Poitiers est annulé.
luh trañ poor pwatyer et anulay
The train to Poitiers is canceled.

5 Say it (2 minutes)

Which platform does the train for Paris leave from?

Three tickets to Lyon, please.

Cultural tip Most train stations have automatic ticket machines that accept credit and debit cards as well as cash.

Ce n'est pas nécessaire. Quarante euros s'il vous plaît.
suh nay pah nesaysair. karont uroh seel voo play

That's not necessary. Forty euros, please.

Vous acceptez les cartes de crédit?
voo zakseptay lay kart duh kredee

Do you accept credit cards?

Bien sûr. Le train part du quai numéro cinq.
byañ syur. luh trañ par doo kay noomairoe sank

Certainly. The train leaves from platform five.

How do you say "train"?
(pp.38-9)

What does "Le train part
de quel quai?" mean?
(pp.38-9)

Ask "When are you
free?" (pp.32-3)

ALLER ET PRENDRE
To go and to take

Aller (*to go*) and **prendre** (*to take*) are essential verbs
in French. You can also use **prendre** to say *I'll have*
(**je prends**) when you talk about food and drink.
Note that the present tense in French includes the
sense of a continuous action–for example, **je vais**
means both *I go* and *I am going*.

2 **Aller: to go** (6 minutes)

Say the different forms of **aller** (*to go*) aloud. Use
the cover flaps to test yourself and, when you are
confident, practice the sample sentences below.

je vais *juh vay*	I go
tu vas *tew vah*	you go (informal singular)
il/elle va *eel/el vah*	he/she goes
nous allons *noo zalloñ*	we go
vous allez *voo zallay*	you go (formal singular or plural)
ils/elles vont *eel/el voñ*	they go

Où allez-vous? *oo allay voo*	Where are you going?
Je vais à Paris. *juh vay zah paree*	I'm going to Paris.
Nous allons à l'école en train. *noo zalloñ ah laykol oñ trañ*	We go to school by train.

Je vais à la Tour Eiffel.
juh vay zah lah toor eefel
I'm going to the
Eiffel Tower.

Cultural tip The **TGV** (**train à grande vitesse**) is a fast train
that can get you from Paris to southern France in about three
hours. Generally you will need to reserve a seat and can
still choose smoking or nonsmoking seats. **TER** (**trains
express régionaux**) is another type of fast train. These
trains are cheaper than the **TGV**. You can buy a ticket
on the day of travel and get on without a reservation.

3 Prendre: to take (6 minutes)

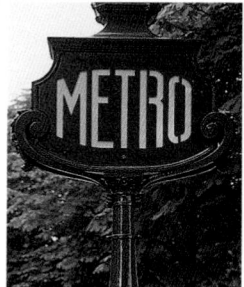

Say the different forms of **prendre** (*to take*) aloud. Use the flaps to cover the French and test yourself. When you are confident, practice the sample sentences below.

je prends *juh proñ*	I take
tu prends *tew proñ*	you take (informal singular)
il/elle prend *eel/el proñ*	he/she takes
nous prenons *noo prunoñ*	we take
vous prenez *voo prunay*	you take (formal singular or plural)
ils/elles prennent *eel/el pren*	they take

Je prends le métro tous les jours.
juh proñ luh metroe too lay joor
I take the metro every day.

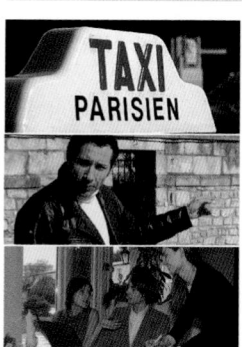

Je ne veux pas prendre un taxi. *juh nuh vuh pah proñdruh uñ taksee*	I don't want to take a taxi.
Prenez la première à gauche. *prunay lah prumyair ah gaush*	Take the first left.
Il prend le bœuf bourguignon. *eel proñ luh buf boorgheenyoñ*	He'll have the beef bourguignon.

4 Put into practice (2 minutes)

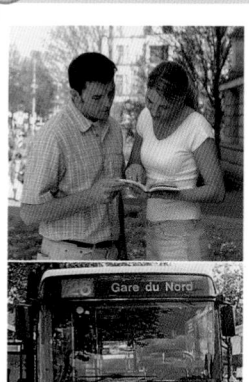

Cover the text on the right and complete the dialogue in French.

Où allez-vous? *oo allay voo* Where are you going?	**Je vais au Louvre.** *juh vay zoh loovruh*
Say: I'm going to the Louvre.	
Vous voulez prendre le métro? *voo voolay proñdruh luh metroe* Do you want to take the metro?	**Non, je veux aller en bus.** *noñ. juh vuh allay oñ boos*
Say: No, I want to go by bus.	

1 Warm up (1 minute)

Say "I'd like to go to the station." (pp.40-1)

Ask "Where are you going?" (pp.40-1)

Say "fruit" and "cheese." (pp.24-5)

TAXI, BUS, ET MÉTRO
Taxi, bus, and metro

With buses, as with trains, you need to validate your ticket in a machine at the time of travel. For the metro, there's a standard fare and you can also buy a **carnet**, a book of 10 tickets. It's unusual to flag down a cab in the street. You need to find one of the many taxi stands and wait there.

2 Words to remember (4 minutes)

Familiarize yourself with these words.

le bus *luh boos*	bus (local)
le car *luh kar*	bus (long-distance)
la gare routière *lah gar rootyair*	bus station
l'arrêt de bus (m) *laray duh boos*	bus stop
le tarif *luh tareef*	fare
le taxi *luh taksee*	taxi
la rangée de taxis *lah roñjay duh taksee*	taxi stand
la station de métro *lah stasyoñ duh metroe*	metro station

Le bus numéro 4 s'arrête ici?
luh boos noomairoe katruh saret eesee
Does the Route 4 bus stop here?

3 In conversation: taxi (2 minutes)

Le marché aux fromages, s'il vous plaît.
luh marshayoe fromarj, seel voo play

The cheese market, please.

Oui, sans problème, monsieur.
wee. soñ problem musyuh

Yes, no problem, sir.

Vous pouvez me déposer ici, s'il vous plaît?
voo poovay muh dayposay eesee, seel voo play

Can you drop me here, please?

4 Useful phrases (4 minutes)

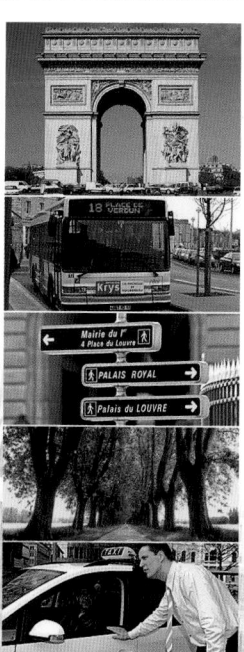

Learn these phrases and then test yourself using the cover flap.

I want a taxi to the Arc de Triomphe.	**Je veux un taxi pour l'Arc de Triomphe.** *juh vuh uh taksee poor lark duh treeoñf*
When is the next bus to the station?	**Quand est le prochain bus pour la gare?** *koñ ay luh proshen boos poor lah gar*
How do you get to the museum?	**Pour aller au musée?** *poor allay oh moozay*
How long is the trip?	**Le trajet dure combien de temps?** *luh trajay dyur koñbyañ duh toñ*
Please wait for me.	**Attendez-moi s'il vous plaît.** *atonday-mwah seel voo play*

Cultural tip Métro lines (**lignes**) in Paris are known by the names of the first and last stations on the line. Follow the signs to the relevant end station—for example, direction Porte d'Orléans. Look out for the beautiful art deco Métropolitain signs retained in some stations.

6 Say it (2 minutes)

Do you go near the train station?

The fruit market, please.

When's the next bus to Calais?

5 In conversation: bus (2 minutes)

Vous allez près du musée?
vooz allay pray doo moozay

Do you go near the museum?

Oui. Ça fait quatre-vingt centimes.
wee. sah fay katruh vañ sonteem

Yes. That's 80 cents.

Dites-moi quand on arrive, s'il vous plaît.
deet mwah koñ toñ areev, seel voo play

Tell me when we arrive, please.

EN ROUTE
On the road

1 Warm up (1 minute)

How do you say "I have…"? (pp.14-15)

Say "my father," "my sister," and "my parents." (pp.16-17)

Say "I'm going to Paris." (pp.40-1)

Be sure to familiarize yourself with the French rules of the road before driving in France. French **autoroutes** (*highways*) are fast but expensive. They are toll (**péage**) roads in which you usually take a ticket as you enter the highway and pay according to the distance traveled as you exit.

2 Match and repeat (4 minutes)

Match the numbered items to the list on the left, then test yourself.

❶ **le coffre**
luh kofrue

❷ **le pare-brise**
luh parbreez

❸ **le capot**
luh kapoh

❹ **le pneu**
luh pnuh

❺ **la roue**
lah roo

❻ **la portière**
lah portyair

❼ **le pare-chocs**
luh parshok

❽ **les phares**
lay far

❶ trunk

wheel ❺

tire ❹

door ❻

Cultural tip Self-service gas stations can be unstaffed. In this case, you usually have to specify how many liters you want and pay by card before filling up.

3 Road signs (2 minutes)

Sens unique
sons ooneek

One way

Rond-point
roñ pwañ

Roundabout

CÉDEZ LE
PASSAGE

Cédez le passage
seday luh passarj

Yield

4 Useful phrases (4 minutes)

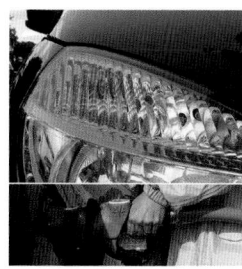

Learn these phrases and then test yourself using the cover flap.

My turn signal doesn't work.	**Mon clignotant ne marche pas.** *moñ kleenyoe-toñ nuh marsh pah*
Fill it up, please.	**Le plein, s'il vous plaît.** *luh plañ, seel voo play*

② windshield

③ hood

headlights **⑧**   **⑦** bumper

5 Words to remember (3 minutes)

Familiarize yourself with these words, then test yourself using the cover flap.

car	**la voiture** *lah vwatyur*
petrol	**l'essence (f)** *laysans*
diesel	**le gazole** *luh gazol*
oil	**l'huile (f)** *lweel*
engine	**le moteur** *luh motur*
gearbox	**la boîte de vitesses** *lah bwat duh veetess*
flat tire	**le pneu crevé** *luh pnuh kruvay*
exhaust	**le pot d'échappement** *luh poe dayshapmoñ*
driver's license	**le permis de conduire** *luh pairmee duh kondweer*

6 Say it (1 minute)

My gearbox doesn't work.

I have a flat tire.

Passage protégé
passarj protayjay

Priority road

Sens interdit
sons añtairdee

Do not enter

Défense de stationner
dayfoñs duh stahseeonay

No parking

Réponses
Answers Cover with flap

RÉVISEZ ET RÉPÉTEZ
Review and repeat

1 Transportation

❶ **le bus**
luh boos

❷ **le taxi**
luh taksee

❸ **la voiture**
lah vwatyur

❹ **le train**
luh trañ

❺ **le vélo**
luh vayloe

❻ **le métro**
luh metroe

1 Transportation (3 minutes)

Name these forms of
transportation in French.

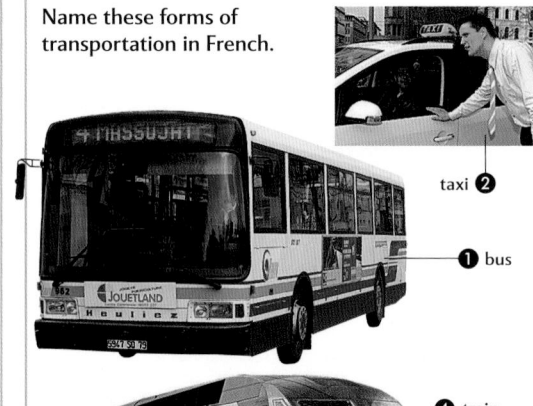

taxi ❷

❶ bus

❹ train

2 Go and take

❶ **allons**
alloñ

❷ **vais**
vay

❸ **prend**
proñ

❹ **allez**
allay

❺ **prenez**
prunay

❻ **prends**
proñ

2 Go and take (4 minutes)

Use the correct form of the
verb in brackets.

❶ Nous _____ à la Tour Eiffel. (aller)

❷ Je _____ à la gare. (aller)

❸ Elle _____ rendez-vous lundi. (prendre)

❹ Où _____-vous? (aller)

❺ Que _____ -vous? (prendre)

❻ Je _____ le bœuf. (prendre)

3 car

5 bicycle

6 metro

METROPOLITAIN

3 Vous or tu?
(4 minutes)

Use the correct form of you.

❶ You are in a café. Ask "Do you have croissants?"

❷ You are with a friend. Ask "Do you want a beer?"

❸ A business woman approaches you at your company reception. Ask "Do you have an appointment?"

❹ You are on the bus. Ask "Do you go near the station?"

❺ Ask your mother where she's going tomorrow.

❻ Ask your client "Are you free on Wednesday?"

Réponses
Answers Cover with flap

3 Vous or tu?

❶ **Vous avez des croissants?**
voo zavay day krossoñ

❷ **Tu veux une bière?**
tew vuh oon biyair

❸ **Vous avez rendez-vous?**
voo zavay roñday voo

❹ **Vous allez près de la gare?**
voo zallay pray duh lah gar

❺ **Où vas-tu demain?**
oo vah-tew dumañ

❻ **Vous êtes libre mercredi?**
voo zet leebruh mairkrudee

4 Tickets (4 minutes)

You're buying tickets at a train station. Follow the conversation, replying in French following the numbered English prompts.

Je peux vous aider?
❶ I'd like two tickets to Lille.

Aller-simple ou aller-retour?
❷ Round-trip, please.

Voilà. Cinquante euros, s'il vous plaît.
❸ What time does the train leave?

A treize heures dix.
❹ What platform does the train leave from?

Quai numéro sept.
❺ Thank you. Goodbye.

4 Tickets

❶ **Je voudrais deux billets pour Lille.**
juh voodray duh beeyay poor leel

❷ **Aller-retour, s'il vous plaît.**
allay rutoor, seel voo play

❸ **A quelle heure part le train?**
ah kel ur par luh trañ

❹ **Le train part de quel quai?**
luh trañ par duh kel kay

❺ **Merci. Au revoir.**
mairsee. ovwar

1 Warm up (1 minute)

Ask "How do you get to the musuem?" (pp.42-3)

Say "I want to take the metro" and "I don't want to take a taxi." (pp.40-1)

EN VILLE
Around town

Most French towns still have a market day and a thriving community of small shops. Even small villages usually have a mayor and a town hall. There may be parking restrictions in downtown areas. Look for signs for **parcmètres** (*pay and display*) and **défense de stationner** (*parking forbidden*).

2 Match and repeat (4 minutes)

Match the numbered locations to the words in the panel.

1 **la mairie**
lah mayree

2 **le pont**
luh poñ

3 **le centre ville**
luh sontruh veel

4 **l'église (f)**
legleez

5 **le parking**
luh parking

6 **la place**
lah plas

7 **la galerie d'art**
lah galree dar

8 **le musée**
luh moozay

church **4**

town hall **1**

bridge **2**

3 Words to remember (4 minutes)

Familiarize yourself with these words and test yourself using the cover flap.

la station service *la stasyoñ servees*	gas station
le syndicat d'initiative *luh sañdeekar deeneesyateev*	tourist information
le garage *luh gararj*	car repair shop
la piscine municipale *lah piseen mooneeseepal*	public swimming pool

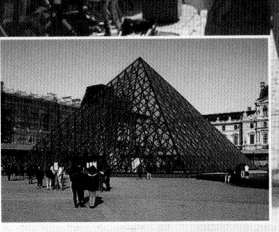

7 art gallery

4 Useful phrases (4 minutes)

La cathédrale est au centre-ville
lah kataydral et oh sontruh veel
The cathedral is downtown.

Learn these phrases and then test yourself using the cover flap.

Is there an art gallery in town?	**Il y a une galerie d'art en ville?** *eelyah oon galree dar oñ veel*
Is it far from here?	**C'est loin d'ici?** *say lwañ deesee*
There is a swimming pool near the bridge.	**Il y a une piscine près du pont.** *eelyah oon piseen pray doo poñ*
There isn't a library.	**Il n'y a pas de bibliothèque.** *eenyah pah duh bib-lee-yotek*

5 Put into practice (2 minutes)

parking lot ❺

❸ downtown

❻ square

museum ❽

Join in this conversation. Read the French on the left and follow the instructions to make your reply. Then test yourself by concealing the answers with the cover flap.

Je peux vous aider? *juh puh voo zeday*	**Il y a une bibliothèque en ville?** *eelyah oon bib-lee-yotek oñ veel*
Can I help you?	
Ask: Is there a library in town?	
Non, mais il ya un musée. *noñ may eelyah uñ moozay*	**Pour aller au musée?** *poor allay oh moozay*
No, but there's a museum.	
Ask: How do I get to the museum?	
C'est là-bas. *say lah bah*	**Merci beaucoup.** *mairsee bohkoo*
It's over there.	
Say: Thank you very much.	

LES DIRECTIONS
Finding your way

1 Warm up (1 minute)

How do you say "near the station"? (pp.42-3)

Say "Take the first left." (pp.40-1)

Ask "Where are you going?" (pp.40-1)

To help you find your way, you'll often find a **plan de la ville** (*town plan*) situated in the town, usually near the town hall or tourist office. In the older parts of French towns there are often narrow streets, in which you will usually find a one-way system in operation. Parking is usually restricted.

2 Useful phrases (4 minutes)

Learn these phrases and then test yourself.

tournez à gauche/droite *toornay ah gaush/dwrat*	turn left/right
sur la gauche/droite *sewr lah gaush/dwrat*	on the right/left
tout droit *too dwrah*	straight ahead
Pour aller à la piscine? *poor allay ah lah piseen*	How do I get to the swimming pool?
la première à gauche *lah prumyair ah gaush*	first left
la deuxième à droite *lah duzyem ah dwrat*	second right

le marché couvert
luh marshay coovair
indoor market

la zone piétonne
lah zohn peeayton
pedestrian zone

Tournez à gauche à la grande place
toornay ah gaush ah lah groñd plas
Turn left at the main square.

3 In conversation (4 minutes)

Il y a un bon restaurant en ville?
eelyah uh boñ restoroñ oñ veel

Is there a good restaurant in town?

Oui, près de la gare.
wee, pray duh lah gar

Yes, near the station.

Pour aller à la gare?
poor allay ah lah gar

How do I get to the station?

4 Words to remember (4 minutes)

Je me suis perdue.
juh muh swee pairdoo
I'm lost.

Familiarize yourself with these words and test yourself using the cover flap.

traffic lights	**les feux**	*lay fuh*
corner	**le coin**	*luh kwañ*
street/road	**la rue**	*lah roo*
main road	**la rue principale**	*lah roo prañseepal*
at the end	**au bout**	*oh boo*
map	**la carte**	*lah kart*
cross	**traversez**	*travairsay*
across from	**en face de**	*oñ fass duh*

le monument
luh moonyumoñ
monument

le plan de la ville
luh plañ duh lah veel
town plan

5 Say it (2 minutes)

Turn right at the end of the street.

It's across from the town hall.

It's ten minutes by bus. .

Tournez à gauche aux feux et puis tout droit.
toornay ah gaush oh fuh ay pwee too dwrah

Turn left at the lights and then straight ahead.

C'est loin?
say lwañ

Is it far?

Non, c'est cinq minutes à pied.
noñ, say sank minoot ah pyay

No, it's five minutes on foot.

LE TOURISME
Sightseeing

1 Warm up (1 minute)

Say the days of the week in French. (pp.28-9)

How do you say "at six o'clock"? (pp.30-1)

Ask "What time is it?" (pp.30-1)

Most national museums close on Tuesdays and public holidays. Although stores are normally closed on Sundays, in tourist areas many will remain open all weekend. It is not unusual, particularly in rural areas, for stores and public buildings to close at lunchtime.

2 Words to remember (4 minutes)

Familiarize yourself with these words and test yourself using the cover flap.

le guide / *luh geed*	guidebook
l'entrée (f) / *loñtray*	entrance ticket
les heures d'ouverture (f) / *lay zur doovairtyur*	opening times
le jour férié / *luh joor fairiyay*	public holiday
l'entrée gratuite (f) / *loñtray gratweet*	free admission

la visite guidée
lah viseet geeday
guided tour

Cultural tip The majority of public buildings and private offices close for public holidays. Many public and private offices are closed in August. If a public holiday falls on a Thursday, the French will often **faire le pont** (*do the bridge*)—in other words, take Friday off to make a long weekend.

3 In conversation (3 minutes)

Vous ouvrez cet après-midi?
voo zoovray set apray-meedee

Do you open this afternoon?

Oui, mais nous fermons à quatre heures.
wee, may noo fairmoñ ah katruh

Yes, but we close at four o'clock.

Vous avez un accès pour les fauteuils roulants?
voo zavay uñ aksay poor lay fohtuhee roolañ

Do you have wheelchair access?

4 Useful phrases (3 minutes)

Learn these phrases and then test yourself using the cover flap.

What time do you open/close?	**Vous ouvrez/fermez à quelle heure?** *voo zoovray/fairmay ah kel ur*
Where is the bathroom?	**Où sont les toilettes?** *oo soñ lay twalet*
Is there wheelchair access?	**Il y a un accès pour les fauteuils roulants?** *eelyah uñ aksay poor lay fohtuhee roolañ*

5 Put into practice (4 minutes)

Cover the text on the right and complete the dialogue in French.

Désolé. Le musée est fermé.
dezolay. luh moozay ay fairmay

Sorry. The museum is closed.

Ask: Do you open on Tuesdays?

Vous ouvrez le mardi?
voo zoovray luh mardee

Oui, mais nous fermons tôt.
wee, may noo fairmoñ toe

Yes, but we close early.

Ask: At what time?

A quelle heure?
ah kel ur

Oui, il y a un ascenseur là-bas.
wee, eelyah uñ asoñsur lah-bah

Yes, there's an elevator over there.

Merci, je voudrais quatre entrées.
mairsee, juh voodray katruh oñtray.

Thank you. I'd like four admission tickets.

Voilà, et le guide est gratuit.
vwalah, ay luh geed ay gratwee

Here you are, and the guidebook is free.

A L'AÉROPORT
At the airport

1 Warm up (1 minute)

Say "You're on time."
(pp.14-15)

What's the French for
"ticket"? (pp.38-9)

Say "I am going to New
York." (pp.40-1)

Although the airport environment is largely universal, it is sometimes useful to be able to ask your way around the terminal in French. It's a good idea to make sure you have a few one-euro coins when you arrive at the airport; you may need to pay for a baggage cart.

2 Words to remember (4 minutes)

l'enregistrement (m) *loñrejeestrumoñ*	check-in
le départ *luh depar*	departures
l'arrivée (f) *lareevay*	arrivals
la douane *lah doo-an*	customs
le contrôle des passeports *luh kontrol day passpor*	passport control
le terminal *luh termee-nal*	terminal
la porte d'embarquement *lah port doñbarkumoñ*	gate
le numéro de vol *luh noomairoe duh vol*	flight number

Familiarize yourself with these words and test yourself using the cover flap.

Quelle est la porte d'embarquement pour le vol numéro vingt-trois?
kel ay lah port doñbarkumoñ poor luh vol numairoh vañ-trwah
What gate does Flight 23 leave from?

3 Useful phrases (3 minutes)

Learn these phrases and then test yourself using the cover flap.

Le vol pour Nice est à l'heure? *luh vol poor nees et ah lur*	Is the flight to Nice on time?
Je ne trouve pas mes bagages. *juh nuh troov pah may bagarj*	I can't find my baggage.
Le vol pour Londres est retardé. *luh vol poor londruh ay retarday*	The flight to London is delayed.

4 Put into practice (3 minutes)

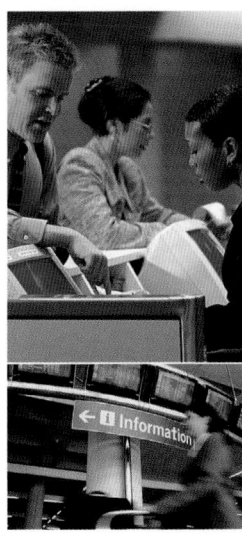

Join in this conversation. Read the French on the left and follow the instructions to make your reply. Then test yourself by concealing the answers with the cover flap.

Bonsoir, monsieur. Je peux vous aider?
boñswar, musyuh. juh puh voo zayday

Good evening, sir. Can I help you?

Ask: Is the flight to Paris on time?

Le vol pour Paris est à l'heure?
luh vol poor paree et ah lur

Oui, monsieur
wee musyuh

Yes, sir.

Ask: What gate does it leave from?

Quelle est la porte d'embarquement?
kel ay lah port doñbarkumoñ

5 Match and repeat (4 minutes)

Match the numbered items to the French words in the panel.

❶ la carte d'embarquement
lah kart doñbarkumoñ

❷ l'enregistrement des bagages (m)
loñrejeestrumoñ day bagarj

❸ le billet
luh beeyay

❹ le passeport
luh passpor

❺ la valise
lah valeez

❻ le bagage à main
luh bagarj ah mañ

❼ le chariot
luh shareeyoh

boarding ❶ pass

baggage ❷ check-in

ticket ❸

passport ❹

❺ suitcase   ❻ carry-on luggage   ❼ cart

Réponses
Answers (Cover with flap)

RÉVISEZ ET RÉPÉTEZ
Review and repeat

Réponses
Answers (Cover with flap)

1 Places

❶ **le musée**
luh moozay

❷ **la mairie**
lah mayree

❸ **le pont**
luh poñ

❹ **la galerie d'art**
lah galree dar

❺ **le parking**
luh parking

❻ **la cathédrale**
lah kataydral

❼ **la place**
lah plas

1 Places (4 minutes)

Name the numbered places in French.

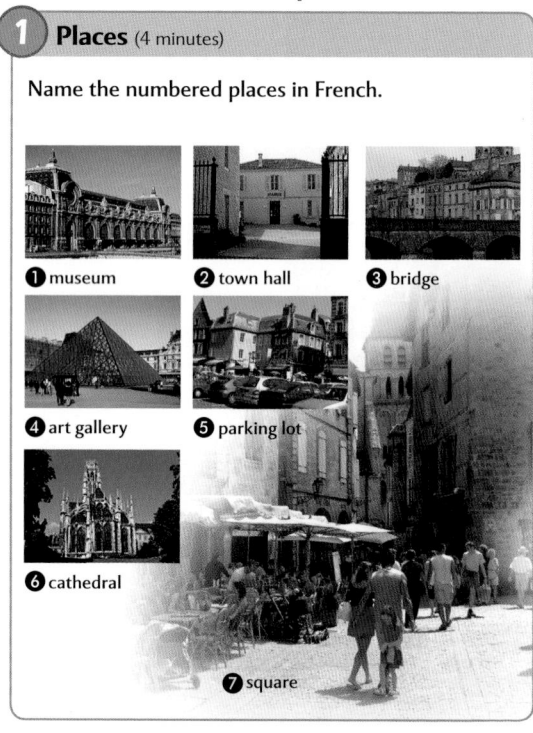

❶ museum ❷ town hall ❸ bridge

❹ art gallery ❺ parking lot

❻ cathedral

❼ square

2 Car parts

❶ **le pare-brise**
luh parbreez

❷ **le clignotant**
luh kleenyoe-toñ

❸ **le capot**
luh kapoh

❹ **le pneu**
luh pnuh

❺ **la portière**
lah portyair

❻ **le pare-chocs**
luh parshok

2 Car parts (3 minutes)

Name these car parts in French.

windshield ❶

❹ tire ❺ door

GETTING AROUND 57

Answers (Cover with flap)

3 Questions (4 minutes)

Ask the questions that match these answers.

1 Le car part à huit heures.
luh kar par ah weet ur

2 Le café, c'est deux euros cinquante.
luh kafay, say duh zuroh sankont

3 Non, je ne veux pas de vin.
noñ. juh nuh vuh pah duh vañ

4 Le train part du quai cinq.
luh trañ par doo kay sank

5 Nous allons à Paris.
noo zalloñ ah paree

6 Non, c'est cinq minutes à pied.
noñ, say sank minoot ah pyay

3 Questions

1 Le car part à quelle heure?
luh kar par ah kel ur

2 C'est combien le café?
say koñbyañ luh kafay

3 Vous voulez du vin?
voo voolay doo vañ

4 Le train part de quel quai?
luh trañ par duh kel kay

5 Où allez-vous?
oo allay voo

6 C'est loin?
say lwañ

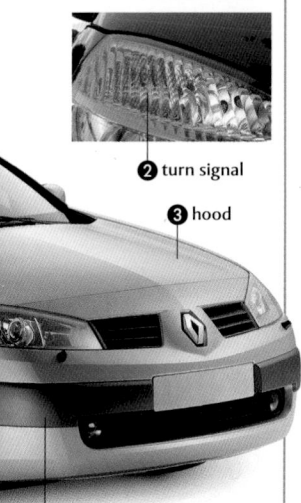

2 turn signal

3 hood

6 bumper

4 Verbs (4 minutes)

Choose the correct words to fill the gaps.

1 Je _____ anglais.

2 Nous _____ le bus.

3 Elle _____ à Paris.

4 Il _____ trois filles.

5 Tu _____ un thé?

6 Combien d'enfants _____ -vous?

7 Je _____ rendez-vous pour mardi.

8 Où _____ les toilettes?

4 Verbs

1 suis
swee

2 prenons
prunoñ

3 va
vah

4 a
ah

5 veux
vuh

6 avez
avay

7 prends
proñ

8 sont
soñ

1 Warm up (1 minute)

How do you ask in French "Do you accept credit cards?" (pp.38-9)

Ask "How much is that?" (pp.18-19)

Ask "Do you have children?" (pp.12-13)

There are different types of accommodation: **l'hôtel**, categorized from one to five stars; **la pension**, a small family-run hotel; and **les chambres d'hôte** (like bed and breakfast) which are often situated in beautiful old properties.

2 Useful phrases (3 minutes)

Practice these phrases and then test yourself by concealing the French on the left with the cover flap.

Le petit-déjeuner est compris?
luh puhtee dayjunay ay koñpree

Is breakfast included?

Vous acceptez les animaux de compagnie?
voo zakseptay lay zanimoe duh koñpañee

Do you accept pets?

Vous avez un room service?
voo zavay uñ room survees

Do you have room service?

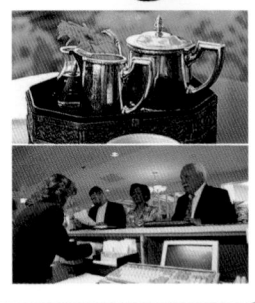

Il faut libérer la chambre à quelle heure?
eel foe leeburay lah shombruh ah kel ur

What time do I have to check out?

3 In conversation (5 minutes)

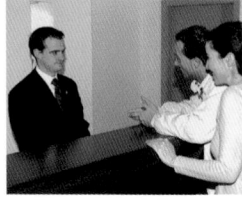

Vous avez des chambres libres?
voo zavay day shombruh leebruh

Do you have any vacancies?

Oui, une chambre double.
wee, oon shombruh doobluh

Yes, a double room.

Vous avez un lit d'enfant?
voo zavay uñ lee doñfoñ

Do you have a crib?

4 Words to remember (4 minutes)

Familiarize yourself with these words and test yourself by concealing the French on the right with the cover flap.

La chambre donne sur le jardin?
lah shombruh don syur luh jardañ
Does the room have a view over the yard?

room	**la chambre** *lah shombruh*
single room	**la chambre simple** *lah shombruh sampluh*
double room	**la chambre double** *lah shombruh doobluh*
twin room	**la chambre twin** *lah shombruh twin*
bathroom	**la salle de bains** *lah sal duh bañ*
shower	**la douche** *lah doosh*
breakfast	**le petit-déjeuner** *luh puhtee dayjunay*
key	**la clé** *lah klay*
balcony	**le balcon** *luh balkoñ*
air-conditioning	**la climatisation** *lah kleematee-zasyoñ*

5 Say it (2 minutes)

Do you have a single room?

Does the room have a balcony?

Cultural tip Chambres d'hôte are usually the only type of accommodation to include breakfast in the price of the room. In other types of hotels, you will usually be charged extra. Many two- or three-star hotels belong to the Logis de France association, which guarantees certain standards of accommodation and service.

Pas de problème. Combien de nuits?
pah duh prob-lem. koñbyañ duh nwee

No problem. How many nights?

Pour trois nuits.
poor trwah nwee

For three nights.

Très bien. Voici la clé.
tray byañ. vwasee lah klay

Very good. Here's the key.

1 Warm up (1 minute)

How do you say "is there...?" and "there isn't..."? (pp.48-9)

What does "Je peux vous aider?" mean? (pp.48-9)

A L'HÔTEL
In the hotel

Although the larger hotels almost always have private bathrooms, there are still some **pensions** and **chambres d'hôte** with shared facilities. This can also be the case in some economy hotels, where a whole family can stay overnight for less than the price of a tank of gas.

2 Match and repeat (6 minutes)

Match the numbered items in this hotel bedroom with the French text in the panel and test yourself using the cover flap.

❶ **la table de chevet**
lah tabluh duh shuvay

❷ **la lampe**
lah lomp

❸ **le mini bar**
luh meeneebar

❹ **les rideaux (m)**
lay reedoe

❺ **le canapé**
luh kanapay

❻ **l'oreiller (m)**
lorayay

❼ **le coussin**
luh koosañ

❽ **le lit**
luh lee

❾ **le dessus de lit**
luh dusoo duh lee

❿ **la couverture**
lah coovurtyur

❹ curtains

❶ nightstand

❺ sofa

❸ mini bar

lamp ❷

❽ bed

❾ bedspread

❿ blanket

❻ pillow   ❼ cushion

Cultural tip When you arrive in your room, you will usually see a long sausage-shaped pillow on the bed called **le traversin**— nowadays a largely decorative item. These are hard and not very comfortable. However, you can usually find square, softer pillows (**les oreillers**) in the cupboard. Do not hesitate to ask if you can't find any.

3 Useful phrases (5 minutes)

Familiarize yourself with these phrases and then test yourself.

The room is too cold/hot.	**La chambre est trop froide/chaude.** *lah shombruh ay troe fwrard/shohd*

There are no towels.	**Il n'y a pas de serviettes.** *eenyah pah duh survyet*

I need some soap.	**J'ai besoin de savon.** *jay buzwañ duh savoñ*

The shower doesn't work very well.	**La douche ne marche pas très bien.** *lah doosh nuh marsh pah tray byañ*

The elevator has broken down.	**L'ascenseur est en panne.** *lasohsur ay toñ pan*

4 Put into practice (3 minutes)

Cover the text on the right and complete the dialogue in French.

Je peux vous aider?
juh puh voo zayday

Can I help you?

Say: I need some pillows.

J'ai besoin d'oreillers.
jay buzwañ dorayay

La femme de chambre va les apporter.
la fam duh shambruh vah lay zaportay

The maid will bring some.

Say: And the television doesn't work.

Et la télévision ne marche pas.
ay lah telayveesyoñ nuh marsh pah

AU CAMPING
At the campground

1 **Warm up** (1 minute)

Ask "Can I?" (pp.34–5)

What is French for "the shower"? (pp.60–1)

Say "I need some towels." (pp.60–1)

Camping is popular in France and there are many well-organized campgrounds. These are rated by a star system. Most towns have **un camping municipal** (*public campground*), and there are also many private sites. Campfires are usually forbidden, but you can often rent a barbecue grill.

2 **Useful phrases** (3 minutes)

Familiarize yourself with these phrases and then test yourself using the cover flap.

Je peux louer un vélo? *juh puh looway uñ vayloe*	Can I rent a bicycle?
C'est de l'eau potable? *say duh loe potabluh*	Is this drinking water?
Les feux de camp sont permis? *lay fuh duh koñ soñ pairmee*	Are campfires allowed?
Les radios sont interdites. *lay radyo soñ añtairdeet*	Radios are forbidden.

Le camping est tranquille
luh komping ay troñkeel
The campground is quiet.

le bureau du camping
luh buroh doo komping
campground office

la poubelle
lah poobel
trash can

le double toit
luh doobluh twah
fly sheet

3 **In conversation:** (5 minutes)

J'ai besoin d'un emplacement pour trois nuits.
jay buzwañ d'uñ oñplasmoñ poor trwah nwee

I need a site for three nights.

Il y en a un près de la piscine.
eelyon ah uñ pray duh lah piseen

There's one near the swimming pool.

C'est combien pour une caravane?
say koñbyañ poor oon karavan

How much is it for a camper trailer?

5 Say it (2 minutes)

I need a site for four nights.

Can I rent a tent?

Where's the electrical hookup?

les toilettes (f)
lay twalet
restrooms

**le branchement
électrique**
*luh bronshmoñ
aylektreek*
electrical hookup

la corde
lah kord
guy rope

le piquet
luh peekay
tent peg

4 Words to remember (4 minutes)

Familiarize yourself with these words and test yourself using the cover flap.

tent	**la tente** *lah tont*
camper trailer	**la caravane** *lah karavan*
camper van	**le camping-car** *luh komping-car*
campground	**le camping** *luh komping*
site	**l'emplacement (m)** *loñplasmoñ*
campfire	**le feu de camp** *luh fuh duh koñ*
drinking water	**l'eau potable (f)** *loe potabluh*
garbage	**les détritus (m)** *lay daytreetoo*
showers	**les douches (f)** *lay doosh*
stove fuel	**le camping-gaz** *luh komping-gaz*
sleeping bag	**le sac de couchage** *luh sak duh koosharj*
air mattress	**le matelas pneumatique** *luh mataylah nyumateek*
groundsheet	**le tapis de sol** *luh tapee duh sol*

Cinquante euros, avec une nuit d'avance.
sankoñt uroh, avek oon nwee davons

Fifty euros, one night in advance.

Je peux louer un barbecue?
juh puh looway uñ barbekyoo

Can I rent a barbecue grill?

Oui, mais vous devez verser des arrhes.
wee, may voo duvay vairsay day zar

Yes, but you must pay a deposit.

1 Warm up (1 minute)

Say "hot" and "cold."
(pp.60-1)

What is the French
for "bathroom" (pp.58-9),
"bed", and "pillow"?
(pp.60-1)

LES DESCRIPTIONS
Descriptions

Adjectives are words used to describe people, things,
and places. In French you generally put the adjective
after the thing it describes—for example, **une chambre
froide** (*a cold room*), but in some cases the adjective
is placed before—for example, **un grand café**
(*a large coffee*).

2 Words to remember (7 minutes)

Adjectives can change slightly depending on whether the
thing described is masculine (**le**), feminine (**la**), or plural (**les**),
but often this affects only the spelling, not the pronunciation.
Below, the masculine spelling is followed by the feminine.
For the plural form, just add a (silent) "s" to the appropriate
masculine or feminine form.

grand/grande *groñ/groñd*	big/tall
petit/petite *puhtee/puhteet*	small
chaud/chaude *shoh/shohd*	hot
froid/froide *fwrah/fwrad*	cold
bon/bonne *boñ/bon*	good
mauvais/mauvaise *movay/movez*	bad
lent/lente *loñ/lont*	slow
rapide/rapide *rapeed/rapeed*	fast
bruyant/bruyante *breeyoñ/breeyont*	noisy
tranquille/tranquille *troñkeel/troñkeel*	quiet
dur/dure *dyuh/dyuh*	hard
mou/molle *moo/moll*	soft
beau/belle *boe/bell*	beautiful
laid/laide *leh/led*	ugly

la haute montagne
lah oht moñtanhyuh
high mountain

la basse colline
lah bas koleen
low hill

la petite maison
lah puhteet mayzon
small house

la vieille église
lah veeyay egleez
old church

**Le village est
très beau.**
luh veelarj ay tray boe
The village is
very beautiful.

3 Useful phrases (4 minutes)

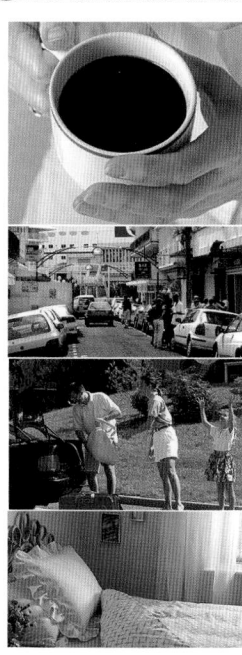

You can emphasize a description by using **très** (*very*), **trop** (*too*), or **plus** (*more*) before the adjective.

This coffee is cold.	**Ce café est froid.** *suh kafay ay fwrah*
My room is very noisy.	**Ma chambre est très bruyante.** *mah shombruh ay tray breeyont*
My car is too small.	**Ma voiture est trop petite.** *mah vwatyur ay troe puhteet*
I need a softer bed.	**J'ai besoin d'un lit plus mou.** *jay buzwañ d'uñ lee ploo moo*

4 Put into practice (3 minutes)

Join in this conversation. Cover up the text on the right and complete the dialogue in French. Check and repeat if necessary.

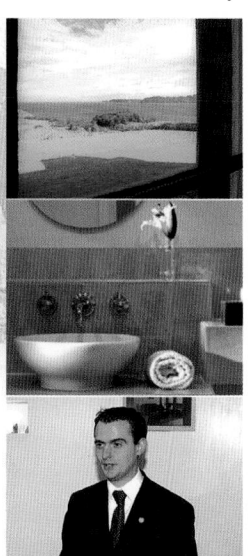

Voici la chambre. *vwasee lah shombruh* Here is the bedroom. Say: The view is very beautiful.	**La vue est très belle.** *lah voo ay tray bell*
La salle de bains est là-bas. *luh sal duh bañ ay lah-bah* The bathroom is over there. Say: It is too small.	**Elle est trop petite.** *el ay troe puhteet*
Nous n'en avons pas d'autre. *noo nañavoñ pah dotruh* We don't have another one. Say: Then we'll take the room.	**Alors nous prenons la chambre.** *Alor noo prunoñ lah shombruh*

RÉVISEZ ET RÉPÉTEZ
Review and repeat

Réponses
Answers (Cover with flap)

1 Adjectives

❶ **chaude**
shohd

❷ **mou**
moo

❸ **bon**
boñ

❹ **petite**
puhteet

❺ **tranquille**
troñkeel

1 Adjectives (3 minutes)

Put the adjective in brackets into French, using the correct masculine or feminine form.

❶ La chambre est trop _____. (hot)

❷ Je voudrais un oreiller plus _____. (soft)

❸ Le café est _____. (good)

❹ Cette salle de bains est trop _____. (small)

❺ Vous avez une chambre plus _____? (quiet)

2 Campground

❶ **le branchement électrique**
luh bronshmoñ aylektreek

❷ **la tente**
lah tont

❸ **la poubelle**
lah poobel

❹ **la corde**
lah kord

❺ **les toilettes**
lay twalet

❻ **la caravane**
lah karavan

2 Campground (3 minutes)

Name these items you might find in a campground.

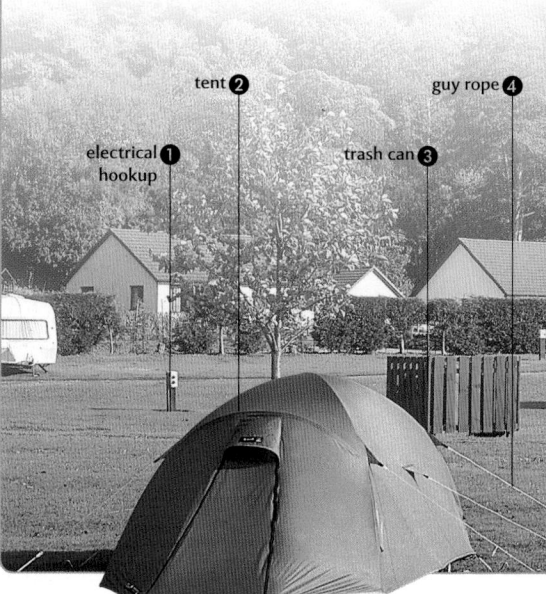

tent ❷

guy rope ❹

electrical ❶ hookup

trash can ❸

3 At the hotel (4 minutes)

You are booking a room in a hotel. Follow the conversation, replying in French following the English prompts.

Je peux vous aider?
❶ Do you have any vacancies?

Oui, une chambre double.
❷ Do you accept pets?

Oui. C'est pour combien de nuits?
❸ Three nights

Ça fait deux cent quarante euros.
❹ Is breakfast included?

Bien sûr, voici la clé.
❺ Thank you very much.

3 At the hotel

❶ **Vous avez des chambres libres?**
voo zavay day shombruh leebruh

❷ **Vous acceptez les animaux de compagnie?**
voo zakseptay lay zanimoe duh koñpañee

❸ **Trois nuits.**
trwah nwee

❹ **Le petit-déjeuner est compris?**
luh puhtee dayjuhnay ay koñpree

❺ **Merci beaucoup.**
mairsee bohkoo

4 Negatives (5 minutes)

Make these sentences negative using the verb in brackets.

❶ Je _____ d'enfants. (avoir)

❷ Elle _____ à Paris demain. (aller)

❸ Il _____ de vin. (vouloir)

❹ Je _____ le train pour Nice. (prendre)

❺ Le café _____ chaud. (être)

4 Negatives

❶ **n'ai pas**
nay pah

❷ **ne va pas**
nuh vah pah

❸ **ne veut pas**
nuh vuh pah

❹ **ne prends pas**
nuh proñ pah

❺ **n'est pas**
nay pah

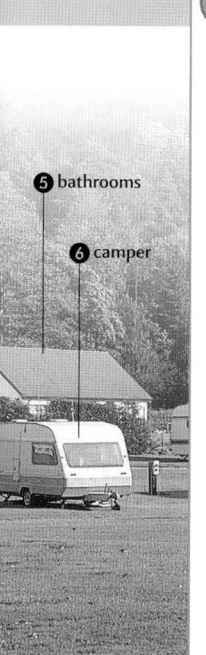

❺ bathrooms

❻ camper

LES MAGASINS
Shops

1 **Warm up** (1 minute)

Ask "How do I get to the station?" (pp.50-1)

Say "Turn left at the traffic lights", "Cross over the street", "The station is opposite the café." (pp.50-1)

In downtown areas, *stores* (**magasins**) are often traditional specialty shops. But you can also find big supermarkets and shopping malls on the outskirts of major towns. Local markets selling fresh, local produce can be found everywhere. You can find out which day is market day at the tourist office.

2 **Match and repeat** (5 minutes)

Match the numbered stores below and right to the French in the panel. Then test yourself using the cover flap.

❶ la boulangerie
lah booloñjuree

❷ la pâtisserie
lah pateesree

❸ le tabac
luh tabah

❹ la boucherie
lah boosheree

❺ la charcuterie
lah sharkooterie

❻ la librairie
lah leebrairee

❼ la poissonnerie
lah pwasoñree

❽ l'épicerie (m)
laypeesree

❾ la banque
lah boñk

❶ bread shop

❷ bakery

❹ butcher shop

❺ delicatessen

❼ fishmonger

❽ grocery store

Cultural tip As well as supplying medicines and health products, a French pharmacy (**pharmacie**) will sell expensive perfume and cosmetics but not generally an everyday bar of soap or a tube of toothpaste. The latter are found at the supermarket or general store. The **tabac** (*tobacconist*) is the place for newspapers and stamps, but also often incorporates a café and bar.

Où est la fleuriste?
oo ay lah flureest
Where is the florist?

3 Words to remember (4 minutes)

Familiarize yourself with these words and test yourself using the cover flap.

hardware store	**la quincaillerie**	*lah kañkayeree*
antique shop	**l'antiquaire (m)**	*lañteekair*
hairdresser	**le coiffeur**	*luh kwafur*
jeweler	**la bijouterie**	*lah bee-jooteree*
post office	**la poste**	*lah post*
shoemaker	**la cordonnerie**	*lah kordoneree*
dry-cleaner	**le pressing**	*luh praysing*
candy store	**le confiseur**	*luh koñfeesur*
cheese shop	**la fromagerie**	*lah fromajeree*

❸ tobacconist

❻ bookshop

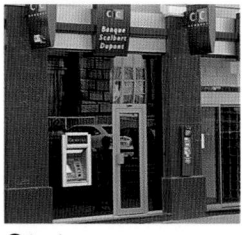

❾ bank

4 Useful phrases (3 minutes)

Familiarize yourself with these phrases.

Where is the hairdresser?	**Où est le coiffeur?**	*oo ay luh kwafur*
Where do I pay?	**Je dois payer où?**	*juh dwah payay oo*
I'm just looking, thank you.	**Je regarde, merci.**	*juh rugard, mairsee*
Do you sell SIM cards?	**Vous vendez des cartes SIM?**	*voo vonday day kart seem*
I'd like two of these.	**J'en veux deux.**	*joñ vuh duh*
Is there a department store in town?	**Il y a un grand magasin en ville?**	*eelyah uñ groñ magazañ oñ veel*
Can I place an order?	**Je peux passer une commande?**	*juh puh passay oon komond*

5 Say it (2 minutes)

Where is the bank?

Do you sell cheese?

Where do I pay?

AU MARCHÉ
At the market

Warm up (1 minute)

What is French for "40", "56", "77", "82", and "94"? (pp.30-1)

Say "I'd like a big room." (pp.64-5)

Ask "Do you have a small car?" (pp.64-5)

France uses the metric system of weights and measures. You need to ask for produce in kilograms or grams. You may find that the older generation still use the term **une livre** (*a pound*) meaning half a kilogram. Some larger items such as melons are sold individually: **à la pièce**.

Match and repeat (4 minutes)

Match the numbered items in this scene with the text in the panel.

❶ **les courgettes** (f)
   lay korjet

❷ **la salade**
   lah sah-lad

❸ **les citrons** (m)
   lay sitroñ

❹ **les poireaux** (m)
   lay pwaroe

❺ **les tomates** (f)
   lay toemat

❻ **les champignons** (m)
   lay shoñpeeyoñ

❼ **les avocats** (m)
   lay zavokah

❽ **les pommes de terre** (f)
   lay pom duh tair

zucchini ❶

❻ mushrooms

tomatoes ❺   potatoes ❽   avocados ❼

In conversation (3 minutes)

Je voudrais des tomates.
juh voodray day toemat

I'd like some tomatoes.

Des grosses ou des petites?
day gros oo day puhteet

The large ones or the small ones?

Deux kilos de grosse, s'il vous plaît.
duh keeloe duh gros, seel voo play

Two kilos of the large ones, please.

Cultural tip France now uses the common European currency, the euro. This is divided into 100 cents, which the French call **centimes** after the old divisions of the franc. You will usually hear the price given as: **dix euros, vingt** (€10.20), **six euros, soixante-treize** (€6.73), etc.

❷ lettuce

❸ lemons

❹ leeks

4 Useful phrases (5 minutes)

Learn these phrases. Then cover the answers on the right. Read the English under the pictures and say the phrase in French as shown on the right.

Le fromage de chèvre est trop cher.
luh fromarj duh shevruh ay troe shair

The goat's cheese is too expensive.

C'est combien ce fromage?
say koñbyañ suh fromarj

How much is that cheese?

Ce sera tout.
suh surah too

That's all.

5 Say it (2 minutes)

Three kilos of potatoes, please.

The mushrooms are too expensive.

How much is the lettuce?

Et avec ceci, madame.
ay avek susee, ma-dam

Anything else, madam.

Ce sera tout, merci. C'est combien?
suh surah too, mairsee. say koñbyañ

That's all, thank you. How much?

Trois euros, cinquante.
trwah zuroh, sankont

Three euros, fifty.

AU SUPERMARCHÉ
At the supermarket

1 Warm up (1 minute)

What are these items you could buy in a supermarket (pp.24–5)?

la viande
le poisson
le fromage
le jus de fruits
le vin
l'eau

Prices in supermarkets are usually lower than in small shops. They offer all kinds of products, with the larger out-of-town **hypermarchés** (*hypermarkets*) extending to clothes, household goods, garden furniture, and home-improvement products. They may also stock regional products.

2 Match and repeat (5 minutes)

Look at the numbered items and match them to the French words in the panel on the left.

❶ **les produits d'entretien (m)**
   lay prodwee doñtruh-tiañ

❷ **les fruits (m)**
   lay froo-wee

❸ **les boissons (m)**
   lay bwassoñ

❹ **les plats préparés (m)**
   lay plah prayparay

❺ **les légumes (m)**
   lay laygoom

❻ **les produits surgelés (m)**
   lay prodwee surjulay

❼ **les produits laitiers (m)**
   lay prodwee letyay

❽ **les produits de beauté (m)**
   lay prodwee duh boetay

household ❶ products

fruit ❷

drinks ❸

prepared ❹ meals

vegetables ❺

frozen foods ❻

Cultural tip Fruit and vegetables sold by the kilo are usually weighed and priced at a separate counter. Alternatively, there may sometimes be a self-service weighing machine.

3 **Useful phrases** (3 minutes)

Learn these phrases and then test yourself using the cover flap.

May I have a bag, please?	**Je peux avoir un sac, s'il vous plaît?** *juh puh avwar uñ sak, seel voo play*
Where is the drinks aisle?	**Où est le rayon des boissons?** *oo ay luh rayonn day bwassoñ*
Where is the check-out, please?	**Où est la caisse, s'il vous plaît?** *oo ay lah kes, seel voo play*
Please type in your PIN.	**Tapez votre code, s'il vous plaît.** *tapay votruh kod, seel voo play*

8 beauty products

7 dairy products

4 **Words to remember** (4 minutes)

Learn these words and then test yourself using the cover flap.

bread	**le pain** *luh pañ*
milk	**le lait** *luh lay*
butter	**le beurre** *luh bur*
ham	**le jambon** *luh joñboñ*
salt	**le sel** *luh sel*
pepper	**le poivre** *luh pwavruh*
laundry detergent	**la lessive** *lah leseev*
toilet paper	**le papier toilette** *luh papyay twalet*
diapers	**les couches (f)** *lay koosh*
dishwashing liquid	**le liquide vaisselle** *luh likeed vaysel*

5 **Say it** (2 minutes)

Where's the dairy products aisle?

May I have some ham, please?

Where are the frozen foods?

VÊTEMENTS ET CHAUSSURES
Clothes and shoes

Say "I'd like..." (pp.22-3)

Ask "Do you have...?" (pp.14-15)

Say "38", "42", and "46." (pp.30-1)

Say "large", "small", "bigger", and "smaller." (pp.64-5)

Clothes and shoes are measured in metric sizes. Even allowing for conversion of sizes, French clothes tend to be cut smaller than American ones. Note that clothes size is **la taille** but shoe size is **la pointure**.

2 Match and repeat (3 minutes)

Match the numbered items of clothing to the French words in the panel on the left. Use the cover flap to test yourself.

1 la chemise
lah shumeez

2 la cravate
lah kravat

3 la veste
lah vest

4 la poche
lah posh

5 la manche
lah moñsh

6 le pantalon
luh poñtaloñ

7 la jupe
lah joop

8 le collants (m)
luh kolloñ

9 les chaussures (f)
lay shohsyur

shirt **1**

tie **2**

jacket **3**

pocket **4**

sleeve **5**

pants **6**

Cultural tip Like most of Europe, France uses the continental system of clothing sizes. Dress sizes usually range from 36 (US 6) through to 46 (US 18) and shoe sizes from 37 (US 6) to 45 (US 12). For men's shirts, a size 41 is a 16-inch collar, 43 is a 17-inch collar, and 45 is an 18-inch collar.

3 Useful phrases (5 minutes)

Learn these phrases and then test yourself using the cover flap.

Do you have a larger size?	**Vous avez une taille plus grande?** *voo zavay oon tie ploo groñd*
It's not what I want.	**Ce n'est pas ce que je veux.** *suh nay pah sukuh juh vuh*
I'll take the pink one.	**Je prends la rose.** *juh proñ lah roz*

4 Words to remember (4 minutes)

Colors are adjectives (pp.64–5) and often have a masculine, feminine, and plural form. The feminine is usually formed by adding an **e** and the plural by adding an **s**.

red	**rouge/rouge** *rooj/rooj*
white	**blanc/blanche** *bloñ/blonsh*
blue	**bleu/bleue** *bluh/bluh*
yellow	**jaune/jaune** *jon/jon*
green	**vert/verte** *vair/vairt*
black	**noir/noire** *nwar/nwar*

⑦ skirt

⑧ pantyhose

⑨ shoes

5 Say it (2 minutes)

I'll take the yellow one.

Do you have this jacket in black?

I'd like a 38.

Do you have a smaller size?

RÉVISEZ ET RÉPÉTEZ
Review and repeat

❶ Market

❶ **les tomates**
lay toemat

❷ **les champignons**
lay shoñpeeyoñ

❸ **les pommes de terre**
lay pom duh tair

❹ **les courgettes**
lay korjet

❺ **la salade**
lah sah-lad

❻ **les avocats**
lay zavokah

❶ Market (3 minutes)

Name the numbered vegetables in French.

❹ zucchini
❶ tomatoes
❷ mushrooms
❺ lettuce
❻ avocados
❸ potatoes

❷ Description

❶ These shoes are too expensive.
❷ My room is very small.
❸ I need a softer bed.

❷ Description (2 minutes)

What do these sentences mean?

❶ **Ces chaussures sont trop chères.**
❷ **Ma chambre est très petite.**
❸ **J'ai besoin d'un lit plus mou.**

❸ Shops

❶ **la boulangerie**
lah booloñjuree

❷ **l'épicerie**
laypeesree

❸ **la librairie**
lah leebrairee

❹ **la poissonnerie**
lah pwasoñree

❺ **la pâtisserie**
lah pateesree

❻ **la boucherie**
lah boosheree

❸ Shops (3 minutes)

Name the numbered shops in French, then check your answers.

❶ bread shop
❷ grocery
❸ bookshop

❹ fishmonger
❺ bakery
❻ butcher

4 Supermarket (3 minutes)

What is the French for the numbered product categories?

1 household products

2 beauty products

3 drinks

4 dairy products

5 frozen foods

4 Supermarket

1 les produits d'entretien
lay prodwee doñtruh-tiañ

2 les produits de beauté
lay prodwee duh boetay

3 les boissons
lay bwassoñ

4 les produits laitiers
lay prodwee letyay

5 les produits surgelés
lay prodwee surjulay

5 Museum (4 minutes)

Follow this conversation replying in French following the English prompts.

Bonjour. Je peux vous aider?
1 Three adults and two children.

Ça fait soixante-dix euros.
2 That's very expensive!

Nous ne faisons pas de réductions pour les enfants.
3 How much is a guide?

Quinze euros.
4 Five tickets and a guide, please.

Quatre-vingt-cinq euros, s'il vous plaît.
5 Here you are. Where are the restrooms?

Là-bas.
6 Thank you very much.

5 Museum

1 Trois adultes et deux enfants.
trwah zadoolt ay duh zoñfoñ

2 C'est très cher!
say tray shair

3 C'est combien pour un guide?
say koñbyañ poor uñ geed

4 Cinq entrées et un guide, s'il vous plaît
sank oñtray ay tuñ geed, seel voo play

5 Voilà. Où sont les toilettes?
vwalah. oo soñ lay twalet

6 Merci beaucoup.
mairsee bohkoo

1 Warm up (1 minute)

Ask "Which platform?"
(pp.38-9)

What is the French for
the following family
members: "sister",
"brother", "mother",
"father", "son", and
"daughter"? (pp.10-11)

OCCUPATIONS
Jobs

Some occupations have a different form when the
person is female—for example, **infirmier** (*male nurse*)
and **infirmière** (*female nurse*). Others, such as
professeur, remain the same for men and women.
When you say your occupation, you don't use
un/une (*a*), as in **Je suis avocat** (*I'm a lawyer*).

2 Words to remember: jobs (7 minutes)

Familiarize yourself with these occupations and test
yourself using the cover flap. The feminine form is
shown in parentheses.

médecin *medsañ*	doctor
dentiste *doñteest*	dentist
infirmier(ière) *añfairmyay(yair)*	nurse
professeur *profesur*	teacher
comptable *koñtabluh*	accountant
avocat(e) *avokah(aht)*	lawyer
designer *deesienur*	designer
consultant(e) *koñsooltoñ(oñt)*	consultant
secrétaire *sekraytair*	secretary
commerçant(e) *komairsoñ(oñt)*	shopkeeper
électricien(ne) *aylektreesyañ(en)*	electrician
plombier *ploñbyay*	plumber
cuisinier(ière) *kweeseenyay(yair)*	cook/chef
ingénieur *añjaynyur*	engineer
à mon compte *ah moñ kont*	self-employed

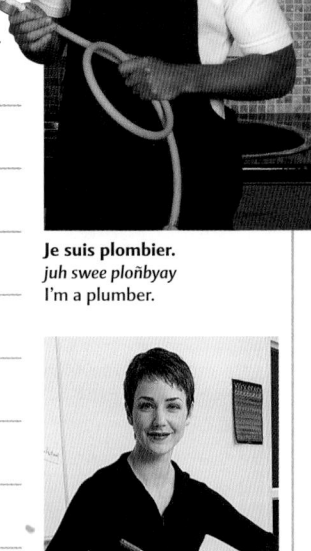

Je suis plombier.
juh swee ploñbyay
I'm a plumber.

Elle est professeur.
el ay profesur
She is a teacher.

3 Put into practice (4 minutes)

Join in the conversation. Conceal the text on the right with the cover flap and complete the dialogue in French.

Quelle est votre profession? *kel ay votruh profesyoñ* What do you do? Say: I am a consultant.	**Je suis consultant.** *juh swee koñsooltoñ*

Vous travaillez pour quelle compagnie? *voo trav-eyeyay poor kel koñpanee* What company do you work for? Say: I'm self-employed.	**Je suis à mon compte.** *juh swee ah moñ kont*

Comme c'est intéressant! *kom say añtayraysoñ* How interesting! Ask: What is your profession?	**Et quelle est votre profession?** *ay kel ay votruh profesyoñ*

Je suis dentiste. *juh swee doñteest* I'm a dentist. Say: My sister is a dentist too.	**Ma sœur est dentiste aussi.** *mah sur ay doñteest ohsee*

4 Words to remember: workplace (3 minutes)

Familiarize yourself with these words and test yourself.

headquarters	**le siège social** *luh syej sosyal*
branch	**lah succursale** *lah sookoorsal*
department	**le département** *luh daypartumoñ*
reception	**la réception** *lah resepsyoñ*
manager	**le chef** *luh shef*
trainee	**le stagiaire** *luh stajyair*

Le siège social est à Lille.
luh syej sosyal ay tah leel
Headquarters is in Lille.

1 Warm up (1 minute)

Practice different ways of introducing yourself in different situations (pp.8–9). Mention your name, occupation, nationality, and any other information you'd like to volunteer.

LE BUREAU
The office

An office environment or business situation has its own vocabulary in any language, but there are many items for which the terminology is virtually universal. Be aware that French computer keyboards have a different layout from the standard English QWERTY convention.

2 Words to remember (5 minutes)

Familiarize yourself with these words. Read them aloud several times and try to memorize them. Conceal the French with the cover flap and test yourself.

French	English
le moniteur *luh moneetur*	monitor
l'ordinateur (m) *lordeenatur*	computer
la souris *lah sooree*	mouse
l'email (m) *leemail*	email
l'internet (m) *lañtairnet*	internet
le mot de passe *luh moh duh pas*	password
la messagerie téléphonique *lah mesah-juree telayfoneek*	voicemail
le code wifi *luh kod weefee*	Wi-Fi code
le copieur *luh kopee-ur*	photocopier
l'agenda (m) *lajeñdah*	planner
la carte de visite *lah kart duh veezeet*	business card
la réunion *lah rayoonyon*	meeting
la conférence *lah konfayroñs*	conference
l'ordre du jour (m) *lordruh doo joor*	agenda

lamp ①

screen ④

laptop ⑥

keyboard ⑤

② stapler

telephone ③

drawer ⑫

pen ⑩   ⑪ notepad

⑦ desk

3 Useful phrases (2 minutes)

Learn these phrases and then test yourself using the cover flap.

I need to make some photocopies.	**J'ai besoin de faire des photocopies.** *jay buzwañ duh fair day fotokopee*
I'd like to arrange an appointment.	**Je voudrais prendre rendez-vous.** *juh voodray proñdruh roñday-voo*
I want to send an email.	**Je veux envoyer un email.** *juh vuh oñvwayay uñ eemail*

4 Match and repeat (5 minutes)

Match the numbered items to the French words on the right.

5 Say it (2 minutes)

I'd like to arrange a conference.

Do you have a business card?

I have a laptop.

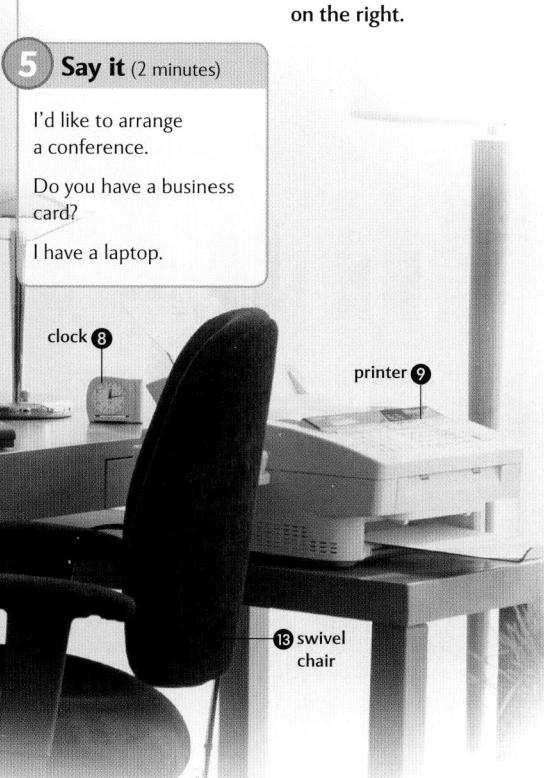

clock **8**

printer **9**

13 swivel chair

❶ **la lampe**
lah lomp

❷ **l'agrafeuse (f)**
lagrafurz

❸ **le téléphone**
luh telayfon

❹ **l'écran (m)**
laykroñ

❺ **le clavier**
luh klaveeyay

❻ **l'ordinateur portable (m)**
lordeenatur portabluh

❼ **le bureau**
luh byuroh

❽ **la pendule**
lah poñdool

❾ **l'imprimante (f)**
lampreemont

❿ **le stylo**
luh steeloh

⓫ **le bloc-notes**
luh blok-not

⓬ **le tiroir**
luh teerwar

⓭ **la chaise tournante**
lah shayz toornont

1 **Warm up** (1 minute)

Say "How interesting!" (p.78-9), "library" (pp.48-9), and "traffic lights." (pp.50-1)

Ask "What is your profession?" and answer "I'm an engineer." (pp.78-9)

LE MONDE ACADÉMIQUE
Academic world

In France, **une licence** (*bachelor's degree*) generally takes three years, followed by **une maîtrise** (*master's degree*) and **un doctorat** (*Ph.D.*). Paris has several universities, often referred to by Roman numerals, as in Paris V.

2 **Useful phrases** (3 minutes)

Familiarize yourself with these phrases and then test yourself.

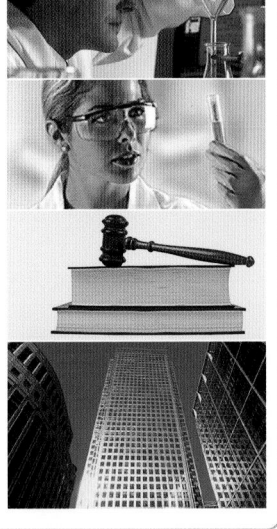

Quel est votre secteur? *kel ay votruh sektur*	What is your field?
Je fais de la recherche en chimie. *juh fay duh lah reshairsh oñ sheemee*	I am doing research in chemistry.
J'ai une licence en droit. *jay oon leesons oñ dwrah*	I have a degree in law.
Je fais une présentation sur l'architecture moderne. *juh fay oon praysoñtasyoñ syur larsheetektur modairn*	I am giving a presentation on modern architecture.

3 **In conversation** (5 minutes)

Bonjour, je suis professeur Stein.
boñjoor, juh swee profesur stayeen

Hello, I'm Professor Stein.

De quelle université êtes-vous?
duh kel ooneevair-sitay et voo

What university are you from?

Je suis déléguée de l'université Paris II.
juh swee daylaygay duh looneevair-sitay paree duh

I'm the delegate from Paris II University.

4 **Words to remember** (4 minutes)

Familiarize yourself with these words and then test yourself.

conference	**la conférence** *lah koñfayroñs*
trade fair	**la foire-exposition** *lah fwar-ekspohseesyoñ*
seminar	**le séminaire** *luh semeenair*
lecture hall	**l'amphithéâtre (m)** *loñfeetayatruh*
conference room	**la salle de conférences** *lah sal duh koñfayroñs*
exhibition	**l'exposition (f)** *lekspohzeesyoñ*
library	**la bibliothèque** *lah biblee-yotek*
assistant professor	**le maître de conférences** *luh metruh duh koñfayroñs*
professor	**le professeur** *luh profesur*
medicine	**la médecine** *lah medseen*
science	**la science** *lah siyons*
literature	**la littérature** *lah leetairatyur*
engineering	**l'ingénierie (f)** *lahjayneeuree*

Nous avons un stand à la foire-exposition.
noo zavon uñ stond ah lah fwar ekspohseesyoñ
We have a stand at the trade fair.

5 **Say it** (2 minutes)

I'm doing research in medicine.

I have a degree in literature.

She's the professor.

Quel est votre secteur?
kel ay votruh sektur

What's your field?

Je fais de la recherche en ingénierie.
juh fay duh lah reshairsh oñ lahjayneeuree

I'm doing research in engineering.

Comme c'est intéressant.
kom say añtayraysoñ

How interesting.

1 **Warm up** (1 minute)

Ask "Can I...?" (pp.34-5)

Say "I want to send an email." (pp.80-1)

Ask "Can you send an email?" (pp.80-1)

LES AFFAIRES
In business

You will receive a more friendly reception and make a good impression if you make the effort to begin a meeting with a short introduction in French, even if your vocabulary is limited. After that, all parties will probably be happy to continue the meeting in English.

2 **Words to remember** (6 minutes)

Familiarize yourself with these words and then test yourself by concealing the French with the cover flap.

le planning *luh planning*	schedule
la livraison *lah leevraysoñ*	delivery
le paiement *luh paymoñ*	payment
le budget *luh bujay*	budget
le prix *luh pree*	price
le document *luh dokoomoñ*	document
la facture *lah faktyur*	invoice
le devis *luh duhvees*	estimate
les bénéfices (m) *lay baynayfees*	profits
les ventes (f) *lay vont*	sales
les chiffres (m) *lay sheefruh*	figures

On signe le contrat?
oñ seenuh luh koñtrah
Shall we sign the contract?

le client
luh kleeyoñ
client

Cultural tip In general, commercial dealings are formal, but a lunch with wine is still part of doing business in France. As a client, you can expect to be taken out to a restaurant, and as a supplier, you should consider entertaining your customers.

3 Useful phrases (6 minutes)

Memorize these phrases. Note that when asking *what...?* you use **quel(s)** with masculine words but **quelle(s)** with feminine words.

Envoyez-moi le contrat s'il vous plaît.
oñvwayay mwah luh koñtrah, seel voo play

Please send me the contract.

le contrat
luh koñtrah
contract

le cadre
luh kadruh
executive

Nous sommes convenus d'un planning?
noo som koñvunoo duñ planning

Have we agreed a schedule?

Quand pouvez-vous faire la livraison?
koñ poovay voo fair lah leevraysoñ

When can you make the delivery?

Quel est le budget?
kel ay luh bujay

What's the budget?

le rapport
luh rapor
report

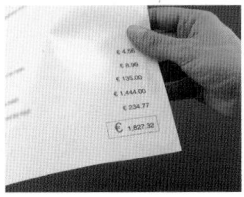

Vous pouvez m'envoyer la facture?
voo poovay moñvwayay lah faktyur

Can you send me the invoice?

4 Say it (2 minutes)

Can you send me the estimate?

Have we agreed on a price?

What are the profits?

Réponses
Answers (Cover with flap)

RÉVISEZ ET RÉPÉTEZ
Review and repeat

1 At the office

❶ **l'agraffeuse**
lagrafurz

❷ **la lampe**
lah lomp

❸ **l'ordinateur portable**
lordeenatur portabluh

❹ **le stylo**
luh steeloh

❺ **le bureau**
luh byuroh

❻ **le bloc-notes**
luh blok-not

❼ **la pendule**
lah poñdool

1 At the office (4 minutes)

Name these items.

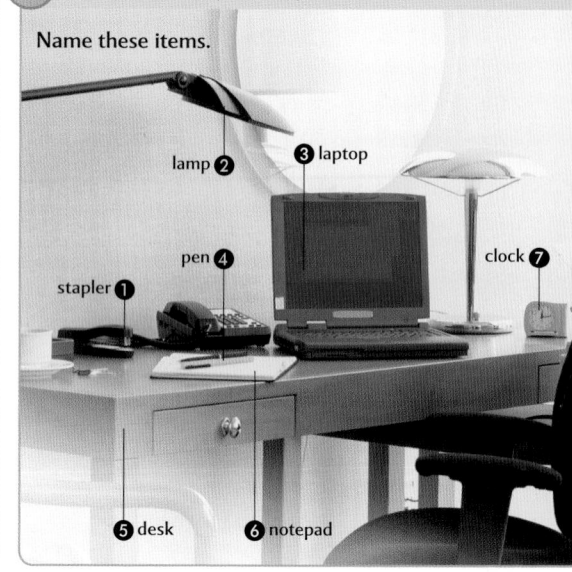

lamp ❷ ❸ laptop
pen ❹   clock ❼
stapler ❶
❺ desk   ❻ notepad

2 Jobs

❶ **médecin**
medsañ

❷ **plombier**
ploñbyay

❸ **commerçant**
comairsoñ(oñt)

❹ **comptable**
koñtabluh

❺ **professeur**
profesur

❻ **avocat**
avokah(aht)

2 Jobs (3 minutes)

What are these jobs in French?

❶ doctor

❷ plumber

❸ shopkeeper

❹ accountant

❺ teacher

❻ lawyer

3 Work (4 minutes)

Answer these questions following the English prompts.

Vous travaillez pour quelle compagnie?
❶ Say "I work for myself."

De quelle université êtes-vous?
❷ Say "I'm at the University of Bordeaux."

Quel est votre secteur?
❸ Say "I'm doing medical research."

Nous sommes convenus d'un planning?
❹ Say "Yes. Can you send me the budget?"

3 Work

❶ **Je suis à mon compte.**
juh swee zah moñ koñt

❷ **Je suis de l'université de Bordeaux.**
juh swee duh looneevair-sitay duh bordoe

❸ **Je fais de la recherche en médecine.**
juh fay duh lah reshairsh oñ medseen

❹ **Oui. Vous pouvez m'envoyer le budget?**
wee. voo poovay moñvwayay lah bujay

4 How much? (4 minutes)

Answer the question with the amount shown in brackets.

❶ **C'est combien le café?** (€2.50)

❷ **C'est combien la chambre?** (€47)

❸ **C'est combien pour un kilo de tomates?** (€3.25)

❹ **C'est combien l'emplacement pour quatre jours?** (€50)

4 How much?

❶ **C'est deux euros cinquante.**
say duh zuroh sankont

❷ **C'est quarante-sept euros.**
say sankont-set uroh

❸ **C'est trois euros vingt-cinq**
say twrah zuroh vañ-sank

❹ **C'est cinquante euros.**
say sankont uroh

① Warm up (1 minute)

Say "I'm allergic to nuts."
(pp.24-5)

Say the verb "avoir" (to
have) in all its forms (je,
tu, il/elle, vous, nous, ils/
elles). (pp.14-15)

A LA PHARMACIE
At the pharmacy

French pharmacists study for seven years before
qualifying. They can give advice about minor
health problems and are permitted to dispense a
wide variety of medicines, even giving injections,
if necessary. There is a duty pharmacist
(**pharmacie de garde**) in most towns.

② Match and repeat (3 minutes)

Match the numbered items to the French
words in the panel on the left and test
yourself using the cover flap.

syrup ②

❶ **le bandage**
  luh boñdarj

bandage ❶

❷ **le sirop**
  luh seeroe

❸ **les gouttes (f)**
  lay goot

❹ **le pansement**
  luh poñsumoñ

⑥ cream

❺ **la seringue**
  lah surañg

❻ **la crème**
  lah krem

drops ❸

❼ **le suppositoire**
  luh soopozitwar

❽ **le cachet**
  luh kashay

adhesive bandage ❹

syringe ❺

③ In conversation (3 minutes)

**Bonjour madame,
vous désirez?**
*boñjoor, mad-dam.
voo dayzeeray*

Hello, madam. What
would you like?

J'ai mal à l'estomac.
jay mal ah lestomah

I have a stomachache.

Vous avez la diarrhée?
voo zavay lah dyaray

Do you have diarrhea?

4 **Words to remember** (2 minutes)

Familiarize yourself with these words and test yourself using the cover flap.

J'ai mal à la tête.
jay mal ah lah tet

I have a headache.

headache	**mal à la tête**	*mal ah lah tet*
stomachache	**mal à l'estomac**	*mal ah lestomah*
diarrhea	**la diarrhée**	*lah dyaray*
cold	**un rhume**	*uñ room*
cough	**une toux**	*oon too*
sunburn	**un coup de soleil**	*uñ koo duh sol-lay*
toothache	**mal aux dents**	*mal oh doñ*

6 **Say it** (2 minutes)

I have a cold.

Do you have that as a cream?

Do you have a cough?

7 suppository

8 tablet

5 **Useful phrases** (4 minutes)

Familiarize yourself with these phrases and then test yourself using the cover flap.

I have sunburn.	**J'ai un coup de soleil.** *jay uñ koo duh sol-lay*
Do you have that as tablets?	**Vous avez des cachets à la place?** *voo zavay day kashay ah lah plas*
I'm allergic to penicillin.	**Je suis allergique à la pénicilline.** *juh swee zalurgeek ah lah peneesilin*

Non, mais j'ai aussi mal à la tête.
noñ, may jay osee mal ah lah tet

No, but I also have a headache.

Prenez ça.
prunay sah

Take this.

Vous avez un sirop à la place?
voo zavay uh seeroe ah lah plas

Do you have that as a syrup?

LE CORPS
The body

The most common phrase for talking about aches and pains is **J'ai mal à...**. Don't forget that when **à** is placed in front of **le** it becomes **au** and in front of **les** it becomes **aux** (the **x** is silent). For example, **J'ai mal au dos** (*I have a backache*) and **J'ai mal aux oreilles** (*I have an earache*).

1 **Warm up** (1 minute)

Say "I have a toothache" and "I have sunburn." (pp.88-9)

Say the French for "red", "green", "black", and "yellow." (pp.74-5)

2 **Match and repeat: body** (6 minutes)

Match the numbered parts of the body with the list on the left. Test yourself by using the cover flap.

1 **la main**
    lah mañ

2 **la tête**
    lah tet

3 **l'épaule (f)**
    laypoll

4 **le coude**
    luh kood

5 **les cheveux**
    lay shuhvuh

6 **le bras**
    luh brah

7 **le cou**
    luh koo

8 **la poitrine**
    lah pwatreen

9 **l'estomac (m)**
    lestomah

10 **la jambe**
    lah jomb

11 **le genou**
    luh juhnoo

12 **le pied**
    luh piyay

1 hand
4 elbow
5 hair
2 head
6 arm
shoulder **3**
7 neck
chest **8**
stomach **9**
leg **10**
knee **11**
12 foot

3 Match and repeat: face (3 minutes)

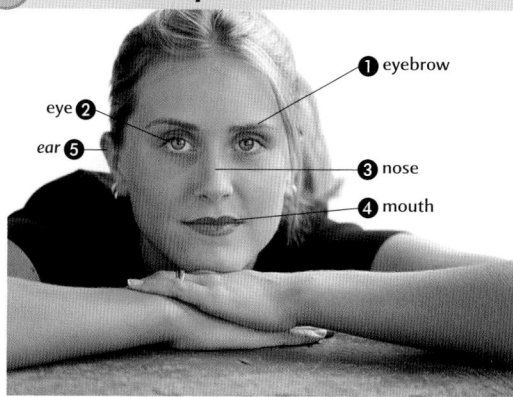

eyebrow
eye ❷
ear ❺
❸ nose
❹ mouth
❶ eyebrow

Match the numbered facial features with the list on the right.

❶ **le sourcil**
luh soorsee

❷ **l'œil (les yeux) (f)**
luhyee (lay zyuh)

❸ **le nez**
luh nay

❹ **la bouche**
lah boosh

❺ **l'oreille (f)**
lor-ray

4 Useful phrases (3 minutes)

Learn these phrases and then test yourself using the cover flap.

I have a pain in my back.
J'ai une douleur au dos.
jay oon doolur oe doh

I have a rash on my arm.
J'ai une rougeur au bras.
jay oon roojur oe brah

I don't feel well.
Je ne me sens pas bien.
juh nuh muh soñ pah byañ

5 Put into practice (2 minutes)

Join in this conversation and test yourself using the cover flap.

Qu'est ce qui ne va pas?
keskee nuh vah pah

Je ne me sens pas bien.
juh nuh muh soñ pah byañ

What's the matter?

Say: I don't feel well.

Tu as mal où?
tew ah mal oo

J'ai une douleur à l'épaule.
jay oon doolur ah laypoll

Where does it hurt?

Say: I have a pain in my shoulder.

CHEZ LE DOCTEUR
At the doctor

1 **Warm up** (1 minute)

Say "I need some tablets" and "He needs some cream." (pp.60-1 and pp.88-9)

What is the French for "I don't have a son"? (pp.10-15)

Unless it's an emergency, you have to make an appointment with the doctor and pay when you leave. You may be able to reclaim the money if you have medical insurance. You can find the names and addresses of local doctors from the local town hall or **syndicat d'initiative** (*tourist office*).

2 **Useful phrases you may hear** (3 minutes)

Familiarize yourself with these phrases and then test yourself using the cover flap to conceal the French on the left.

Ce n'est pas sérieux. *suh nay pah seryuh*	It's not serious.
Vous avez besoin de tests. *voo zavay buzwañ duh test*	You need to have tests.
Vous avez une infection aux reins. *voo zavay oon añfeksyoñ oh rañ*	You have a kidney infection.
Vous avez besoin d'aller à l'hôpital. *voo zavay buzwañ dalay ah lopeetal*	You need to go to hospital.

Vous prenez des médicaments?
voo prunay day maydikamoñ
Are you taking any medications?

3 **In conversation** (5 minutes)

Qu'est-ce qui ne va pas?
keskee nuh vah pah

What's the matter?

J'ai une douleur à la poitrine.
jay oon doolur ah lah pwatreen

I have a pain in my chest.

Laissez-moi vous examiner.
lessay-mwah voo zekzaminay

Let me examine you.

4 Useful phrases you may need to say (4 minutes)

Practice these phrases and then test yourself using the cover flap.

I'm diabetic.	**Je suis diabétique.** *juh swee diyabeteek*
I'm epileptic.	**Je suis épileptique.** *juh swee zepeelepteek*
I'm asthmatic.	**Je suis asthmatique.** *juh swee zasmateek*
I have a heart condition.	**J'ai un problème au cœur.** *jay uñ prob-lem* *oh kur*
I feel faint.	**Je vais m'évanouir.** *juh vay mayvanooweer*
I have a fever.	**J'ai de la fièvre.** *jay duh lah fyevruh*
It's urgent.	**C'est urgent.** *say turjoñ*

Je suis enceinte.
juh swee zoñsant
I'm pregnant.

Cultural tip
Before you go, find out if your health insurance covers emergency medical care in Europe; if it doesn't, buy a travel medical insurance policy. To call an ambulance in France, dial 112.

5 Say it (2 minutes)

Do I need tests?

My son needs to go to hospital.

It's not urgent.

C'est sérieux?
say seryuh

Is it serious?

Non, vous avez seulement une indigestion.
noñ, voo zavay surlmoñ
oon añdeejestyoñ

No, you only have indigestion.

Quel soulagement!
kel soolarjemoñ

What a relief!

1 Warm up (1 minute)

Ask "How long is the trip?" (pp.42-3)

How do you ask "Do I need...?" (pp.92-3)

What is the French for "mouth" and "head"? (pp.90-1)

A L'HÔPITAL
At the hospital

The main hospitals in France are attached to universities and are known as **Centres Hospitaliers Universitaires** (CHU). It is useful to know a few basic phrases relating to hospitals for use in an emergency or in case you need to visit a friend or colleague in the hospital.

2 Useful phrases (5 minutes)

Familiarize yourself with these phrases. Conceal the French with the cover flap and test yourself.

Quelles sont les heures de visite? *kel soñ lay zur duh vizeet*	What are the visiting hours?
Ça va prendre combien de temps? *sah vah prondruh koñbyañ duh toñ*	How long will it take?
Ça va faire mal? *sah vah fair mal*	Will it hurt?
Allongez-vous ici, s'il vous plaît. *aloñjay voo zeesee, seel voo play*	Please lie down here.
Vous ne devez pas manger. *voo nuh duvay pah moñjay*	You must not eat.
Ne bougez pas la tête. *nuh boojay pah lah tet*	Don't move your head.
Ouvrez la bouche, s'il vous plaît. *oovray lah boosh, seel voo play*	Please open your mouth.
Vous avez besoin d'une prise de sang. *voo zavay buzwañ doon preez duh soñ*	You need a blood test.

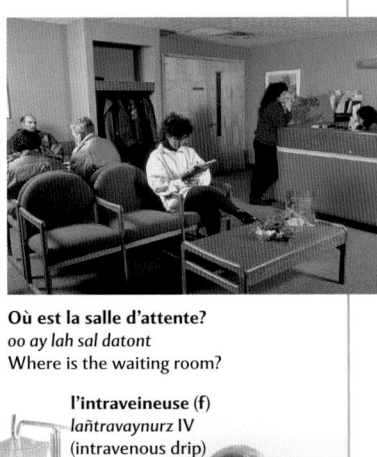

Où est la salle d'attente?
oo ay lah sal datont
Where is the waiting room?

l'intraveineuse (f)
lañtravaynurz IV
(intravenous drip)

Ça va mieux?
sah vah meeyuh
Are you feeling better?

3 **Words to remember** (4 minutes)

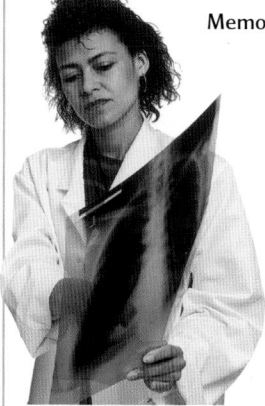

Memorize these words and test yourself using the cover flap.

emergency room	**la salle des urgences** *lah sal day zurjoñs*
children's ward	**le service de pédiatrie** *luh survees duh paydyah-tree*
operating room	**la salle d'opération** *lah sal dopairasyoñ*
X-ray department	**la salle de radiologie** *lah sal duh radyo-lojee*
waiting room	**la salle d'attente** *lah sal datont*
elevator	**l'ascenseur** *lasoñsur*
stairs	**les escaliers** *lay zeskalyay*

Votre radio est normale.
votruh radyoh ay normal
Your X-ray is normal.

4 **Put into practice** (3 minutes)

Join in this conversation. Read the French on the left and follow the instructions to make your reply. Then test yourself by concealing the answers with the cover flap.

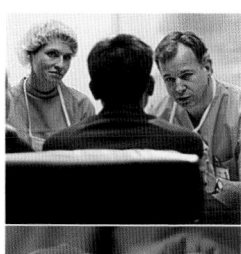

Vous avez une infection.
voo zavay oon añfeksyoñ

You have an infection.

Ask: Do I need tests?

J'ai besoin de tests?
jay buzwañ duh test

Tout d'abord, vous avez besoin d'une prise de sang.
too dabor, voo zavay buzwañ doon preez duh soñ

First you will need a blood test.

Ask: Will it hurt?

Ça va faire mal?
sah vah fair mal

5 **Say it** (2 minutes)

Does he need a blood test?

Where is the children's ward?

Do I need an X-ray?

Non, ne vous inquiétez pas.
noñ, nuh voo zañkyatay pah

No. Don't worry.

Ask: How long will it take?

Ça va prendre combien de temps?
sah vah prondruh koñbyañ duh toñ

Réponses
Answers (Cover with flap)

RÉVISEZ ET RÉPÉTEZ
Review and repeat

1 The body

❶ la tête
lah tet

❷ le bras
luh brah

❸ la poitrine
lah pwatreen

❹ l'estomac
lestomah

❺ la jambe
lah jomb

❻ le genou
luh juhnoo

❼ le pied
luh piyay

1 The body (4 minutes)

Name the numbered body parts in French.

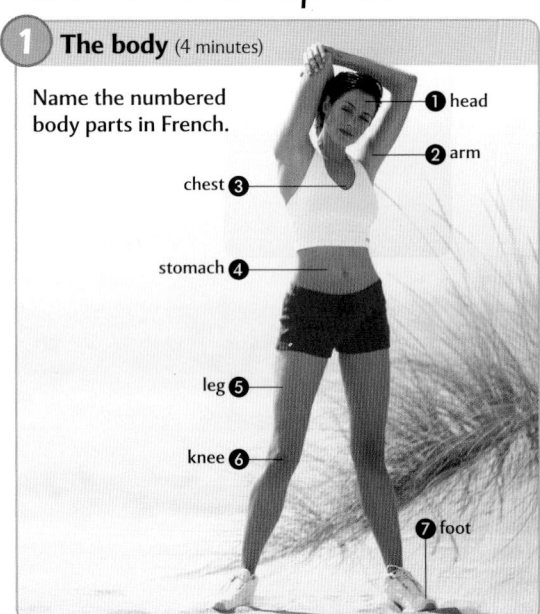

❶ head
❷ arm
chest ❸
stomach ❹
leg ❺
knee ❻
❼ foot

2 On the phone

❶ Je voudrais parler à Caroline Martin.
juh voodray parlay ah karoleen martañ

❷ [your name] de l'imprimerie Laporte.
[your name] duh lahpreemuree laport

❸ Je peux laisser un message?
juh puh laysay uñ mesarj

❹ C'est bon pour le rendez-vous lundi à onze heures.
say boñ poor luh roñday-voo lañdee ah onz ur

❺ Merci, au revoir.
mairsee, ovwar

2 On the phone (4 minutes)

You are arranging an appointment. Follow the conversation, replying in French following the English prompts.

Allô, société Apex.
❶ I'd like to speak to Caroline Martin.

Oui, c'est de la part de qui?
❷ [your name] of Laporte printers.

Je suis désolé, la ligne est occupée.
❸ Can I leave a message?

Oui, bien sûr.
❹ The appointment on Monday at 11 am is fine.

Très bien, au revoir.
❺ Thank you. Goodbye.

3 Clothing (3 minutes)

Say the French words for the numbered items of clothing.

tie ❶
❷ jacket
❹ skirt
pants ❸
❻ pantyhose
shoes ❺

3 Clothing

❶ **la cravate**
lah kravat

❷ **la veste**
lah vest

❸ **le pantalon**
luh poñtaloñ

❹ **la jupe**
lah joop

❺ **les chaussures**
lay shohsyur

❻ **les collants**
lay kolloñ

4 At the doctor's (4 minutes)

Say these phrases in French.

❶ I don't feel well.
❷ Do I need tests?
❸ I have a heart condition.
❹ Do I need to go to hospital?
❺ I am pregnant.

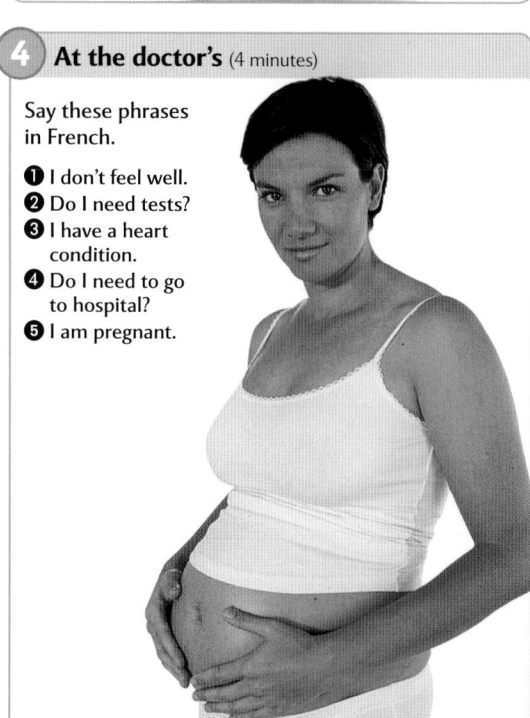

4 At the doctor's

❶ **Je ne me sens pas bien.**
juh nuh muh soñ pah byañ

❷ **J'ai besoin de tests.**
jay buzwañ duh test

❸ **J'ai un problème au cœur.**
jay uñ prob-lem oh kur

❹ **J'ai besoin d'aller à l'hôpital.**
jay buzwañ dallay ah lopeetal

❺ **Je suis enceinte.**
juh swee zoñsant

1 Warm up (1 minute)

Say the months of the year in French. (pp.28-9)

Ask "Is there an art gallery?" (pp.48-9) and "How many brothers do you have?" (pp.14-15)

CHEZ NOUS
At home

Many city-dwellers live in an apartment block (**l'immeuble**), but in rural areas the houses tend to be single-family (**individuelle**). If you want to know the total number of rooms, you will need to ask "**Combien de pièces?**" If you want to know how many bedrooms, ask "**Combien de chambres?**"

2 Match and repeat (5 minutes)

Match the numbered items to the list and test yourself using the cover flap.

❶ **la fenêtre**
lah fenaytruh

❷ **la cheminée**
lah shemnay

❸ **le toit**
lah twut

❹ **la gouttière**
lah gootyair

❺ **le mur**
luh myur

❻ **le volet**
luh volay

❼ **la porte**
lah port

❽ **le passage**
luh passarj

chimney ❷

window ❶

❺ wall   ❻ shutter

Cultural tip Most French houses have shutters (**volets**) at each window. These are closed at night and in the heat of the day. Curtains, where they are present, tend to be more for decoration. A single-story bungalow is known as **un pavillon**, and these are popular among the French as vacation homes in tourist resorts.

3 **Words to remember** (4 minutes)

Quel est le loyer par mois?
kel ay luh lwayay par mwah?
What is the rent per month?

Familiarize yourself with these words and test yourself using the cover flap.

room	**la pièce**	*lah piyes*
floor	**le sol**	*luh sol*
ceiling	**le plafond**	*luh plafoñ*
bedroom	**la chambre**	*lah shombruh*
bathroom	**la salle de bains**	*lah sal duh bañ*
kitchen	**la cuisine**	*lah kwiseen*
dining room	**la salle à manger**	*lah sal ah moñjay*
living room	**le salon**	*luh saloñ*
basement	**la cave**	*lah kav*
attic	**le grenier**	*luh grunyay*

3 roof

4 gutter

4 **Useful phrases** (3 minutes)

Learn these phrases and test yourself.

Is there a garage?

Il y a un garage?
eelyah uh gararj

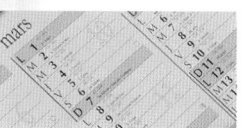
When is it available?

C'est disponible quand?
say deesponeebluh koñ

Is it furnished?

C'est meublé?
say murblay

8 driveway   door **7**

5 **Say it** (2 minutes)

Is there a dining room?

Is it large?

Is it available in July?

DANS LA MAISON
In the house

What is the French for "room" (pp.58-9), "desk" (pp.80-1), "bed" (pp.60-1), and "bathroom(s)"? (pp.52-3)

How do you say "soft", "beautiful", and "big"? (pp.64-5)

When you rent a house or villa in France, it is usual to be asked to pay for services such as electricity and gas in addition to the basic weekly or monthly rent. Additional charges might also extend to wood or other fuel for an open fire, which is usually charged by the cubic meter.

2 **Match and repeat** (3 minutes)

Match the numbered items to the list in the panel on the left. Then test yourself by concealing the French with the cover flap.

1 **le plan de travail**
luh plañ duh traveye

2 **l'évier (m)**
levyay

3 **le micro-ondes**
luh meekro-ond

4 **la cuisinière**
lah kwiseenyair

5 **le four**
luh foor

6 **le frigo**
luh freegoh

7 **la table**
lah tabluh

8 **la chaise**
lah shez

4 stove   **1** countertop   **6** refrigerator   chair **8**   **5** oven   table **7**

3 **In conversation** (3 minutes)

C'est le four.
say luh foor

This is the oven.

Il y a un lave-vaisselle aussi?
eelyah uñ lav-vaysel osee

Is there a dishwasher as well?

Oui, et il y a un grand congélateur.
wee, ay eelyah uñ groñ koñjelatur

Yes, and there's a big freezer.

4 **Words to remember** (2 minutes)

Familiarize yourself with these words and test yourself using the cover flap.

Le canapé est neuf.
luh kanapay ay nurf
The sofa is new.

wardrobe	**l'armoire (f)** *larmwar*
armchair	**le fauteuil** *luh fohtuhee*
chest of drawers	**la commode** *lah komohd*
fireplace	**la cheminée** *lah shemnay*
carpet	**le tapis** *luh tapee*
bathtub	**la baignoire** *lah bainwar*
bathroom sink	**le lavabo** *luh lavabo*
curtains	**les rideaux (m)** *lay ridoe*

❷ sink   microwave ❸

6 **Say it** (2 minutes)

Is there a microwave?

I like the fireplace.

What a soft sofa!

5 **Useful phrases** (4 minutes)

Practice these phrases and then test yourself using the cover flap to conceal the French.

Is electricity included?	**L'électricité est inclue?** *laylektreesitay et añkloo*
I don't like the curtains.	**Je n'aime pas les rideaux.** *juh nem pah lay ridoe*
The carpet is old.	**Le tapis est vieux.** *luh tapee ay vyuh*

L'évier est neuf?
levyay ay nurf

Is the sink new?

Bien sûr. Et voilà la machine à laver.
byañ syur. ay vwalah lah masheen ah lavay

Of course. And here's the washing machine.

Quel beau carrelage!
kel boe karlarj

What beautiful tiles!

LE JARDIN
The backyard

1 Warm up (1 minute)

Say "I need", "you need", "he needs." (pp.64-5, pp.92-4)

What is the French for "day", "week", and "month"? (pp.28-9)

Say the days of the week. (pp.28-9)

The yard of a house or villa may be communal, or at least partly shared. Check with the rental agent or realtor. In general, French yards are well-kept and reasonably formal. The natural, "wild" look is not very popular and hedges are usually carefully trimmed and lawns regularly mown.

2 Words to remember (3 minutes)

Familiarize yourself with these words and test yourself using the cover flap.

la tondeuse à gazon *lah toñdurz ah gazoñ*	lawnmower
la fourche *lah foorsh*	fork
la bêche *lah besh*	spade
le râteau *luh ratoe*	rake
la jardinerie *lah jardañree*	garden center

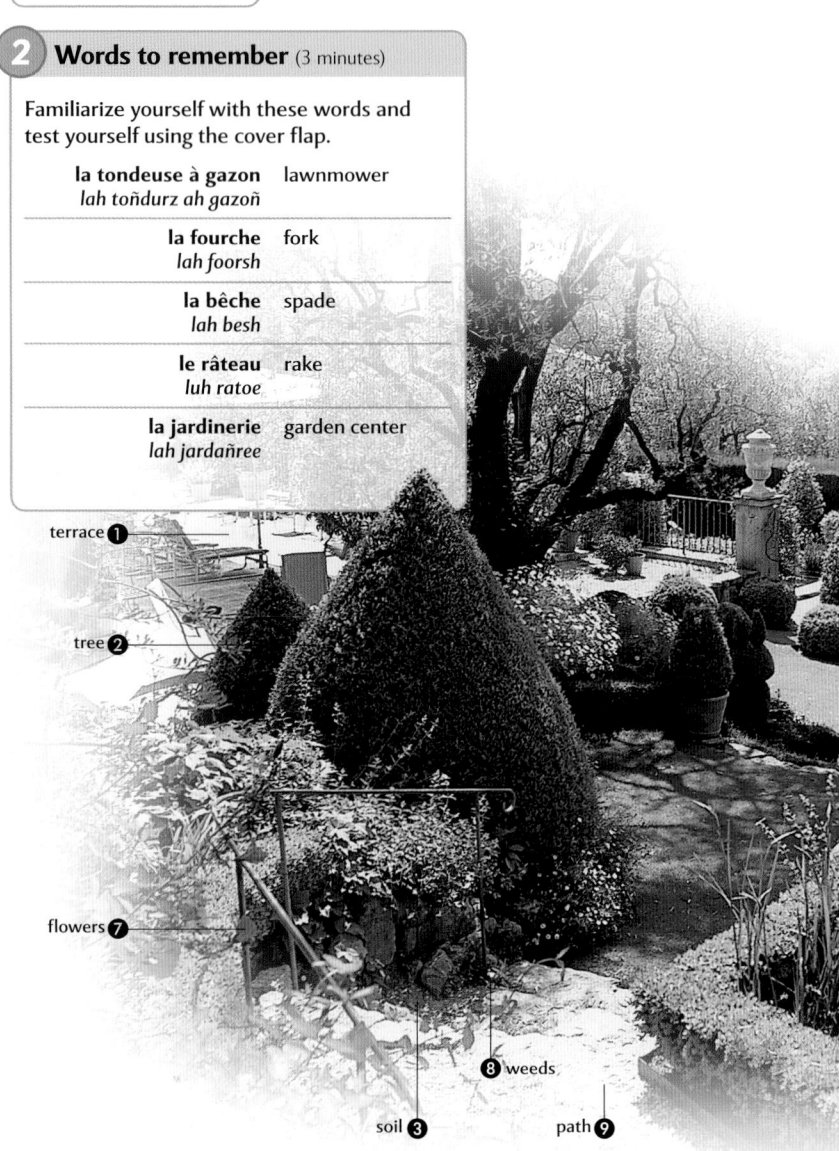

terrace ➊

tree ➋

flowers ➐

➑ weeds

soil ➌

path ➒

3 Useful phrases (4 minutes)

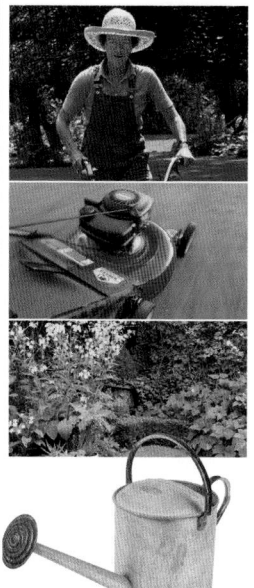

Familarize yourself with these phrases and then test yourself.

The gardener comes once a week.	**Le jardinier vient une fois par semaine.** *luh jardañyay vyañ oon fwah par suhmayn*
Can you mow the lawn?	**Vous pouvez tondre la pelouse?** *voo poovay toñdruh lah pelooz*
Is the yard private?	**Le jardin est privé?** *luh jardañ ay preevay*
The yard needs watering.	**Le jardin a besoin d'eau.** *luh jardañ ah buzwañ doe*

⑤ hedge

④ lawn

4 Match and repeat (5 minutes)

Match the numbered items to the words in the panel on the right.

❶ la terrasse
lah terass

❷ l'arbre (m)
larbruh

❸ la terre
lah tair

❹ la pelouse
lah pelooz

❺ la haie
lah ay

❻ les plantes (f)
lay ploñt

❼ les fleurs (f)
lay flur

❽ les mauvaises herbes (f)
lay movay zurb

❾ l'allée (f)
lallay

❿ le parterre de fleurs
luh partair duh flur

5 Say it (2 minutes)

The lawn needs watering.

Are there any trees?

The gardener comes on Fridays.

❻ plants

❿ flower bed

LES ANIMAUX
Pets

Half of all French households include at least one pet, and most companion animals are treated like members of the family. There are slightly more pet dogs than pet cats in France. Fish and birds are also widely kept, and rabbits and rodents are becoming increasingly popular.

1 Warm up (1 minute)

Say "My name's John." (pp.8-9)

How do you say "don't worry"? (pp.94-5)

What's "your" in French? (pp.12-13)

2 Match and repeat (3 minutes)

Match the numbered animals to the French words in the panel on the left. Then test yourself using the cover flap.

1 le chat
luh shah

2 le lapin
luh lapañ

3 l'oiseau (m)
lwazoe

4 le poisson
luh pwassoñ

5 le chien
luh shiañ

6 le hamster
luh amstair

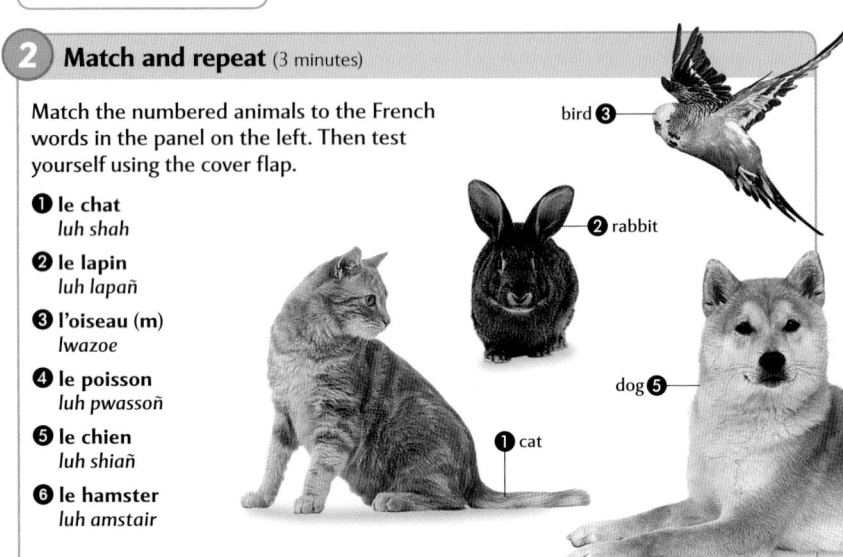

bird **3**

2 rabbit

dog **5**

1 cat

3 Useful phrases (4 minutes)

Familiarize yourself with these phrases and then test yourself using the cover flap.

Ce chien est gentil? *suh shiañ ay joñtee*	Is this dog friendly?
Je peux amener mon chien? *juh puh amunay moñ shiañ*	Can I bring my dog?
J'ai peur des chats. *jay pur day shah*	I'm afraid of cats.
Mon chien ne mord pas. *moñ shiañ nuh mor pah*	My dog doesn't bite.

Ce chat est plein de puces.
suh shah ay plañ duh pous
This cat is full of fleas.

Cultural tip Many dogs in France are guard dogs, and you may encounter them tethered or roaming free. Approach farms and rural houses with care, and keep away from the dog's territory. Look out for warning notices such as **Attention au chien** (*Beware of the dog*).

ATTENTION AU CHIEN

Mon chien est malade.
moñ shiañ ay malahd
My dog is not well.

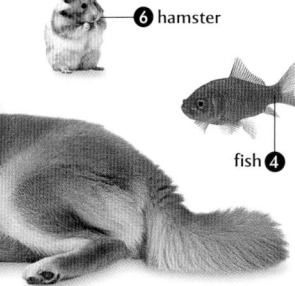

⑥ hamster

fish ④

4 Words to remember (4 minutes)

Memorize these words and test yourself using the cover flap.

vet	**le vétérinaire** *luh vetairinair*
vaccination	**la vaccination** *lah vaksinasyoñ*
pet passport	**le passeport d'animaux** *luh passpor danimoe*
basket	**le panier** *luh panyay*
cage	**la cage** *lah karj*
bowl	**la gamelle** *lah gamel*
collar	**le collier** *luh kolyay*
leash	**la laisse** *lah less*
fleas	**les puces (f)** *lay pous*

5 Put into practice (3 minutes)

Join in this conversation. Read the French on the left and follow the instructions to make your reply. Then test yourself by concealing the answers with the cover flap.

C'est votre chien?
say votruh shiañ

Is this your dog?

Say: Yes, his name is Sandy.

Oui, il s'appelle Sandy.
wee, eel sapell Sandy

J'ai peur des chiens.
jay pur day shiañ

I'm afraid of dogs.

Say: Don't worry. He's friendly.

Ne vous inquiétez pas. Il est gentil.
nuh voo zañkyatay pah. eel ay joñtee

Réponses
Answers (Cover with flap)

RÉVISEZ ET RÉPÉTEZ
Review and repeat

1 Colors

❶ noir
nwar

❷ blanche
blonsh

❸ rouge
rooj

❹ verte
vairt

❺ jaunes
jon

1 Colors (4 minutes)

Complete the sentences with the French for the color in brackets. Be careful to choose the correct masculine or feminine form.

❶ Vous avez cette veste en _____? (black)

❷ Je prends la jupe _____. (white)

❸ Vous avez cette robe en _____? (red)

❹ Non mais j'ai une _____. (green)

❺ Vous avez des chaussettes _____? (yellow)

2 Kitchen

❶ la cuisinière
lah kwiseenyair

❷ le frigo
luh freegoh

❸ l'évier
levyay

❹ le micro-ondes
luh meekro-ond

❺ le four
luh foor

❻ la chaise
lah shez

❼ la table
lah tabluh

2 Kitchen (4 minutes)

Say the French words for the numbered items.

stove ❶   refrigerator ❷

❺ oven   chair ❻

3 House (4 minutes)

You are visiting a house in France. Join in the conversation, replying in French following the English prompts.

Voilà le salon.
❶ What a pretty fireplace!

Oui, et il y a aussi une grande cuisine.
❷ How many bedrooms?

Il y a trois chambres.
❸ Do you have a garage?

Non, mais il y a un grand jardin.
❹ When is it available?

Juillet.
❺ What is the rent per month?

3 House

❶ **Quelle belle cheminée!**
kel bel shemnay

❷ **Combien de chambres?**
koñbyañ duh shombruh

❸ **Vous avez un garage?**
voo zavay uñ gararj

❹ **C'est disponible quand?**
say deesponeebluh koñ

❺ **Quel est le loyer par mois?**
kel ay luh lwayay par mwah

4 At home (3 minutes)

Say the French for the following items:

❶ washing machine
❷ sofa
❸ attic
❹ dining room
❺ tree
❻ yard

microwave ❹
❸ sink
table ❼

4 At home

❶ **la machine à laver**
lah masheen ah lavay

❷ **le canapé**
luh kanapay

❸ **le grenier**
luh grunyay

❹ **la salle à manger**
lah sal ah moñjay

❺ **l'arbre**
larbruh

❻ **le jardin**
luh jardañ

1 Warm up (1 minute)

Ask "How do I get to the bank?" and "How do I get to the post office?" (pp.68-9)

What's the French for "passport"? (pp.54-5)

Ask "What time?" (pp.30-1)

LA POSTE ET LA BANQUE
Post office and bank

The post office also serves as a bank. You do not usually need to wait in line for a teller, since there are normally ATMs available outside the building. Stamps are also available from **le tabac** (*bar/tobacconists*).

2 Words to remember: mail (3 minutes)

la boîte postale *lah bwat post-tal*	mailbox
la carte postale *lah kart post-tal*	postcard
le colis *luh kolee*	package
par avion *par avyoñ*	air mail
en recommandé *oñ rukomoñday*	registered mail
le timbre *luh tambruh*	stamp
le code postal *luh kod post-tal*	postal (ZIP) code
le facteur *luh faktur*	mail carrier

Familiarize yourself with these words and test yourself using the cover flap to conceal the French on the left.

C'est combien pour le Royaume-Uni?
say koñbyañ poor luh royom oonee
How much is it for the United Kingdom?

l'enveloppe (f)
loñvuhlop
envelope

3 In conversation (3 minutes)

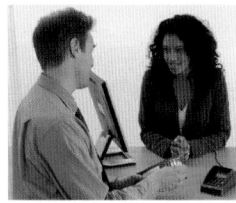

Je voudrais retirer de l'argent.
juh voodray ruteeray duh larjoñ

I'd like to withdraw some money.

Vous avez une identification?
voo zavay oon eedoñtee-fikasyoñ

Do you have any identification?

Oui, voilà mon passeport.
wee, vwalah moñ passpor

Yes, here's my passport.

la carte bancaire
lah kart boñkair
debit card

Comment je peux payer?
komon juh puh payay
How can I pay?

4 Words to remember: bank (2 minutes)

Familiarize yourself with these words and test yourself using the flap to conceal the French on the right.

PIN	**le code** *luh kod*	
bank	**la banque** *lah boñk*	
teller	**le guichet** *luh geeshay*	
notes	**les billets** *lay beeyay*	
ATM	**le distributeur automatique** *luh distreebootur otomateek*	
credit card	**la carte de crédit** *lah kart duh kraydee*	

5 Useful phrases (4 minutes)

Learn these phrases and then test yourself using the cover flap.

I'd like to change some money.	**Je voudrais changer de l'argent.** *juh voodray shoñjay duh larjoñ*
What is the exchange rate?	**Quel est le taux de change?** *kel ay luh toe duh shoñj*
I'd like to withdraw some money.	**Je voudrais retirer de l'argent.** *juh voodray ruteeray duh larjoñ*

6 Say it (2 minutes)

I'd like a stamp for a postcard.

Can I pay by credit card?

Do I need my PIN?

Composez votre code s'il vous plaît.
komposay votruh kod seel voo play

Please type in your PIN.

J'ai besoin de signer aussi?
jay buzwañ duh seenyay ohsee

Do I need to sign, too?

Non, ce n'est pas nécessaire.
noñ, suh nay pah nesesair

No, that's not necessary.

1 **Warm up** (1 minute)

What's the French for
"doesn't work"?
(pp.60-1)

Say "today" and
"tomorrow." (pp.28-9)

LES SERVICES
Services

You can combine the French words on these pages
with the vocabulary you learned in week 10 to help
you explain basic problems and cope with arranging
most repairs. When negotiating building work or a
repair, it's a good idea to agree on the price and
method of payment in advance.

2 **Words to remember** (4 minutes)

Familiarize yourself with these words and test
yourself using the cover flap.

le plombier *luh ploñbyay*	plumber
l'électricien (m) *laylektreesyañ*	electrician
le garagiste *luh gararjeest*	mechanic
le constructeur *luh koñstruktur*	builder, handyman
la femme de ménage *lah fam duh maynarj*	cleaner
le décorateur *luh daykoratur*	decorator
le charpentier *luh sharpañtyay*	carpenter
le maçon *luh massoñ*	bricklayer

la manivelle
lah maneevel
tire iron

Je n'ai pas besoin d'un garagiste.
juh nay pah buzwañ duñ gararjeest
I don't need a mechanic.

3 **In conversation** (3 minutes)

**La machine à laver est
en panne.**
*lah masheen ah lavay ay
toñ pan*

The washing machine has
broken down.

**Oui, le tuyeau
est cassé.**
*wee luh tweeyoh
ay kassay*

Yes, the hose is broken.

**Vous pouvez
la réparer?**
voo poovay lah rayparay

Can you repair it?

4 Useful phrases (3 minutes)

Learn these phrases and then test yourself using the cover flap.

Please clean the bathroom.	**Nettoyez la salle de bain, s'il vous plait.** *netwuhyay lah sal duh bañ seel voo play*
Can you repair the boiler?	**Vous pouvez réparer la chaudière?** *voo poovay rayparay lah shodyair*
Do you know a good electrician?	**Vous connaissez un bon électricien?** *voo konessay uñ boñ aylektreesyañ*

Je peux faire réparer ça où?
juh puh fair rayparay sah oo
Where can I get this repaired?

5 Put into practice (4 minutes)

Practice these phrases. Cover up the text on the right and complete the dialogue in French. Check your answers and repeat if necessary.

Votre clôture est cassée. *votruh klotoor ay kassay* Your fence is broken. Ask: Do you know a good handyman?	**Vous connaissez un bon constructeur?** *voo konessay uh boñ koñstruktur*
Oui, il y en a un dans le village. *wee, eelyonah uñ doñ luh villarj* Yes, there is one in the village. Ask: Do you have his phone number?	**Vous avez son numéro de téléphone?** *voo zavay soñ noomairoe duh telayfon*

Non, vous avez besoin d'un nouveau.
noñ. voo zavay buzwañ duñ noovoh

No, you need a new one.

Vous pouvez faire ça aujourd'hui?
voo poovay fair sah oh-joordwee

Can you do it today?

Non, je reviens demain.
non, juh ruvyañ dumañ

No. I'll come back tomorrow.

VENIR
To come

1 Warm up (1 minute)

Say the days of the week in French. (pp.28-9)

How do you say "cleaner"? (pp.110-11)

Say "It's 9:30," "10:45," and "12:00." (pp.10-11, pp.30-1)

The verb **venir** (*to come*) is another important verb. Other useful verbs are made up of **venir** with a prefix, such **revenir** (*to come back*) and **devenir** (*to become*). These can be formed in the same way as **venir** (below). Remember that **je viens** can mean either *I come* or *I am coming*.

2 Venir: to come (6 minutes)

Say the different forms of **venir** (*to come*) aloud. Use the cover flap to test yourself and, when you are confident, practice the sample sentences below.

je viens *juh vyañ*	I come
tu viens *tew vyañ*	you come (informal singular)
il/elle vient *eel/el vyañ*	he/she comes
nous venons *noo vunoñ*	we come
vous venez *voo vunay*	you come (formal singular or plural)
ils/elles viennent *eel/el vyen*	they come
Je viens de New York. *juh vyañ duh noo york*	I come from New York.
Nous venons tous les mardis. *noo vunoñ too lay mardee*	We come every Tuesday.
Ils viennent par le train. *eel vyen par luh trañ*	They come by train.

Il vient de Chine.
eel vyañ duh sheen
He comes from China.

Conversational tip You can use the phrase **je viens de...** (literally *I come from...*) to talk about something you have just done or have recently completed—for example, **je viens de faire les courses** (*I have just gone shopping*) or **je viens d'envoyer un email** (*I have just sent an email*). To say *just* in the sense of *only*, as in *I eat just a sandwich for lunch*, the French use **seulement**: **Je mange seulement un sandwich pour déjeuner**.

③ Useful phrases (4 minutes)

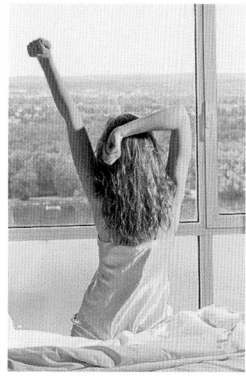

Je viens de me réveiller.
juh vyañ duh muh rayvay-yay
I have just woken up.

Learn these phrases and then test yourself using the cover flap.

When can I come?	**Je peux venir quand?** *juh puh vuneer koñ*
Where does she come from?	**Elle vient d'où?** *el vyañ doo*
The cleaner comes every Monday.	**La femme de ménage vient tous les lundis.** *lah fam duh maynarj vyañ too lay luñdee*
Come with me. (informal/formal)	**Viens avec moi./ Venez avec moi.** *vyañ avek mwah/ vunay avek mwah*

④ Put into practice (4 minutes)

Join in this conversation. Read the French on the left and follow the instructions to make your reply. Then test yourself by concealing the answers with the cover flap.

Bonjour, salon de coiffure Christine.
boñjoor, saloñ duh kwafur Christine

Hello, this is Christine's hair salon.

Say: I'd like an appointment.

Je voudrais un rendez-vous.
juh voodray uñ roñday-voo

Vous voulez venir quand?
voo voolay vuneer koñ

When do you want to come?

Say: Can I come today?

Je peux venir aujourd'hui?
juh puh vuneer oh-joordwee

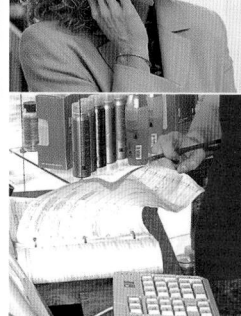

Oui bien sûr, à quelle heure?
wee byañ syur, ah kel ur

Yes, of course. What time?

Say: At 10:30.

A dix heures et demie.
ah deez ur ay dumee

1 Warm up (1 minute)

What's the French for "big/tall" and "small/short"? (pp.64-5)

Say "The room is big" and "The bed is small." (pp.64-5)

LA POLICE ET LE CRIME
Police and crime

While in France, if you are the victim of a crime, you report it to the police. In an emergency, reach them by dialing 112. You may have to explain your problem in French, at least initially, so some basic vocabulary is useful. In the event of a burglary, the police will usually come to the house.

2 Words to remember: crime (4 minutes)

Familiarize yourself with these words.

J'ai besoin d'un avocat.
jay buzwañ duñ avokah
I need a lawyer.

le cambriolage *luh kañbryolarj*	burglary
le rapport de police *luh rapor duh polees*	police report
le voleur *luh volur*	thief
la police *lah polees*	police
la déposition *lah daypoziyoñ*	statement
le témoin *luh taymwañ*	witness
l'avocat(e) *lavokah(aht)*	lawyer

3 Useful phrases (3 minutes)

Memorize these phrases and then test yourself using the cover flap.

J'ai été cambriolé(e). *jay aytay kañbryolay*	I've been burgled.
Qu'est-ce qui a été volé? *keskee ah aytay volay*	What was stolen?
Vous avez vu qui a fait ça? *voo zavay voo kee ah fay sah*	Did you see who did it?
Ça s'est passé quand? *sah say passay koñ*	When did it happen?

l'appareil-photo
lapareye foto
camera

le porte-monnaie
luh port mohnay
wallet

4 Words to remember: appearance (5 minutes)

Learn these words. Remember, some adjectives have a feminine form.

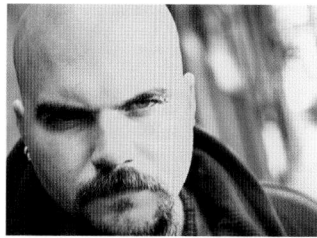

Il est chauve avec une barbe.
eel ay shohv avek oon barb
He is bald and has a beard.

Il a les cheveux noirs et courts.
eel ah lay shuvuh nwar ay kor
He has short, black hair.

man	**l'homme (m)** *lom*
woman	**la femme** *lah fam*
tall	**grand/grande** *groñ/groñd*
short	**petit/petite** *puhtee/puhteet*
young	**jeune** *juhn*
old	**vieux/vieille** *vyuh/vyay*
fat	**gros/grosse** *groe/gros*
thin	**maigre** *maygruh*
long/short hair	**les cheveux longs/ courts (m)** *lay shuvuh loñ/kor*
glasses	**les lunettes (f)** *lay loonet*
beard	**la barbe** *lah barb*

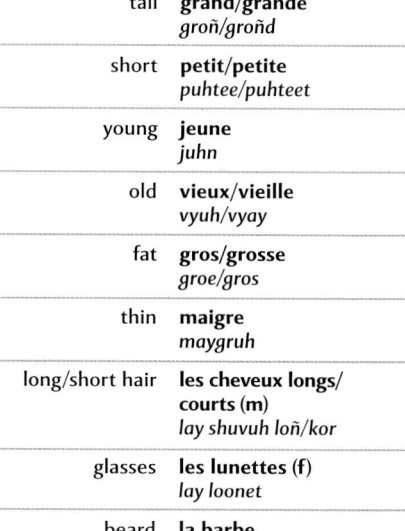

Cultural tip In France there is a difference between **la gendarmerie** and **la police**. **La gendarmerie** operates in smaller towns and **la police** in major cities. Their appearance and uniform are similar and officers from both forces carry guns.

5 Put into practice (2 minutes)

Practice these phrases. Then cover the text on the right and follow the instructions to make your reply in French.

Il ressemblait à quoi?   **Petit et gros.**
eel ruzoñblay ah kwah   *puhtee ay groe*

What did he look like?

Say: Short and fat.

Et les cheveux?   **Longs avec une barbe.**
ay lay shuvuh   *loñ avek oon barb*

And the hair?

Say: Long, with a beard.

Réponses
Answers (Cover with flap)

RÉVISEZ ET RÉPÉTEZ
Review and repeat

❶ To come

❶ **viviens**
vyañ

❷ **vient**
vyañ

❸ **venons**
vunoñ

❹ **venez**
vunay

❺ **viennent**
vyen

❶ To come (3 minutes)

Fill in the blanks with the correct form of **venir** (*to come*).

❶ Je _____ à quatre heures.

❷ Le jardinier _____ une fois par semaine.

❸ Nous _____ pour déjeuner mardi.

❹ Vous _____ avec nous?

❺ Mes parents _____ par le train.

❷ Bank and mail

❶ **le colis**
luh kolee

❷ **les timbres**
lay tambruh

❸ **les cartes postales**
lay kart post-tal

❹ **les billets**
lay biyay

❺ **la carte bancaire**
lah kart boñkair

❷ Bank and mail (4 minutes)

Say the French words for the following numbered items:

stamps ❷

❶ package

postcards ❸

❹ notes

❺ bank card

3 Appearance (4 minutes)

What do these descriptions mean?

❶ C'est un homme grand et maigre.

❷ Elle a les cheveux courts et des lunettes.

❸ Je suis petite et j'ai les cheveux longs.

❹ Elle est vieille et grosse.

❺ Il a les yeux bleus et une barbe.

3 Appearance

❶ He's a tall, thin man.

❷ She has short hair and glasses.

❸ I'm short and I have long hair.

❹ She is old and fat.

❺ He has blue eyes and a beard.

4 The pharmacy (4 minutes)

You are asking a pharmacist for advice. Join in the conversation, replying in French following the English prompts.

Bonjour. Je peux vous aider?
❶ I have a cough.

Et vous avez aussi un rhume?
❷ No, but I have a headache.

Prenez ces cachets.
❸ Do you have that as a syrup?

Bien sûr. Voilà.
❹ Thank you. How much is that?

Six euros.
❺ Here you are. Goodbye.

4 The pharmacy

❶ J'ai une toux.
jay oon too

❷ Non, mai j'ai mal à la tête.
noñ. may jay mal ah lah tet

❸ Vous avez un sirop à la place?
voo zavay uñ seeroe ah lah plas

❹ Merci. C'est combien?
mairsee. say koñbyañ

❺ Voilà. Au revoir.
vwalah. ovwar

1 Warm up (1 minute)

What is the French for "museum" and "art gallery"? (pp.48-9)

Say "I don't like the curtains." (pp.100-1)

Ask "Do you want...?" informally. (pp.22-3)

LES LOISIRS
Leisure time

The French pride themselves on their support for the arts, including opera and film. It would not be unusual to number politics or philosophy among your interests. Phrasebooks aimed at French speakers often have a section on useful conversational openers for these topics.

J'adore l'opéra.
jador lopayra
I love opera.

2 Words to remember (4 minutes)

Familiarize yourself with these words and test yourself using the cover flap to conceal the French on the left.

le théâtre *luh tay-atruh*	theater
le cinéma *luh sinaymah*	movie theater
la discothèque *lah diskotek*	disco
la musique *lah moozeek*	music
l'art (m) *lar*	art
le sport *luh spor*	sports
le tourisme *luh torizmuh*	sightseeing
les jeux vidéos *lay juh viday-oh*	computer games

3 In conversation (4 minutes)

Salut, tu veux jouer au tennis aujourd'hui?
saloo, tew vuh jooay oh tenees oh-joordwee

Hi, do you want to play tennis today?

Non. Je n'aime pas le sport.
noñ. juh nem pah luh spor

No, I don't like sports.

Alors, quels sont tes intérêts?
alor, kel soñ tay zañtairay

So what are your interests?

Je déteste la guitare.
juh daytest lah geetar
I hate guitar music.

les spectateurs (m)
lay spektahtur
audience

4 Useful phrases (4 minutes)

Learn these phrases and then test yourself using the cover flap.

What are your (formal/informal) interests?	**Quels sont vos/tes intérêts?** *kel soñ voe/tay zañtayray*
I like the theater.	**J'aime le théâtre.** *jem luh tay-atruh*
I prefer the movies.	**Je préfère le cinéma.** *juh prayfair luh sinaymah*
I'm interested in art.	**Je m'intéresse à l'art.** *juh mañtairess ah lar*
That bores me.	**Ça m'ennuie.** *sah moñwee*

la galerie
lah galuree
balcony

l'orchestre (m)
lorkestruh
orchestra

5 Say it (2 minutes)

I'm interested in music.

I prefer sports.

I don't like computer games.

Je préfère le shopping.
juh prayfair luh shopping

I prefer shopping.

Ça ne m'intéresse pas.
sah nuh mañtairess pah

That doesn't interest me.

Pas de problème. J'y vais toute seule.
pah de prob-lem. jee vay toot surl

No problem. I'll go on my own.

LE SPORT ET LES PASSE-TEMPS
Sport and hobbies

1 **Warm up** (1 minute)

Ask "Do you (formal) want to play tennis?" (pp.118-19)

Say "I like the theater" and "I prefer sightseeing." (pp.118-19)

Say "That doesn't interest me." (pp.118-19)

The verb **faire** (to do or to make) is a useful verb for talking about hobbies. **Faire** is followed by **du, de la** or **de l':** **Je fais de la peinture** (I paint). You can also use the verb **jouer** (to play) when talking about playing sports and music.

2 **Words to remember** (5 minutes)

Memorize these words and then test yourself.

le football/rugby *luh futbohl/roogbee*	soccer/rugby
le tennis *luh tenees*	tennis
la natation *lah natasyoñ*	swimming
la voile *lah vwal*	sailing
la pêche *lah pesh*	fishing
la peinture *lah pañtyur*	painting
le vélo *luh vaylo*	cycling
la randonnée *lah rañdonay*	hiking

le bunker
luh bañkuh
bunker

le joueur de golf
luh joowur duh golf
golfer

Je joue au golf tout les jours.
juh joo oh golf too lay joor
I play golf every day.

3 **Useful phrases** (2 minutes)

Familiarize yourself with these phrases.

Je fais du rugby. *juh fay doo roogbee*	I play rugby.
Il joue au tennis. *eel joo oh tenees*	He plays tennis.
Elle fait de la peinture. *el fay duh lah pañtyur*	She paints.

4 Faire: to do or to make (4 minutes)

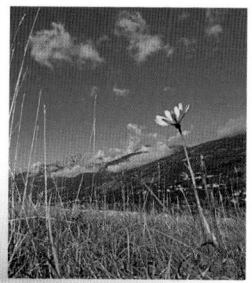

The verb **faire** (*to do* or *to make*) is also used to describe the weather. Learn its different forms and practice the sample sentences below.

I do	**je fais** *juh fay*
you do (informal)	**tu fais** *tew fay*
he/she does	**il/elle fait** *eel/el fay*
we do	**nous faisons** *noo fayzon*
you do (formal/plural)	**vous faites** *voo fet*
they do	**ils/elles font** *eel/el foñ*
I go hiking.	**Je fais de la randonnée.** *juh fay duh lah rañdonay*
What do you do?	**Que faites-vous?** *kuh fet voo*
We play tennis.	**Nous faisons du tennis.** *noo fayzon doo tenees*

Il fait beau aujourd'hui.
eel fay boe oh-joordwee
It's nice out today.

___ **le drapeau**
luh drapoh
flag

_____ **le parcours de golf**
luh parkoor duh golf
golf course

5 Put into practice (3 minutes)

Practice these phrases. Then cover up the text on the right and complete the dialogue in French. Check your answers.

Qu'est-ce que vous aimez faire?
keskuh voo zemay fair

What do you like doing?

Say: I like playing tennis.

J'aime jouer au tennis.
jem jooway oh tenees

Tu fais du football aussi?
tew fay doo futbohl ohsee

Do you play soccer, too?

Say: No. I play rugby.

Non, je fais du rugby.
noñ, juh fay doo roogbee

Cultural tip France boasts a huge variety of regional games, such as pelota in the Basque country. Most popular of all, the French version of bowls—**pétanque** or **boules**—is played in almost every town and village.

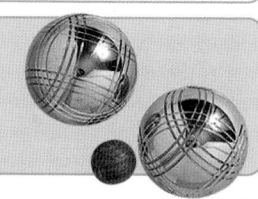

VOIR DES GENS
Socializing

1 Warm up (1 minute)

Say "my husband" and "my wife." (pp.10-11)

How do you say "lunch" and "dinner" in French? (pp.20-1)

Say "Sorry, I'm busy." (pp.32-3)

The French dinner table is the center of the social world. You can expect to do a lot of your socializing enjoying food and wine. It is best to use the more polite **vous** form to talk to people you meet socially until they call you **tu**, in which case you can reciprocate.

l'invitée (f)
lanveetay
guest

2 Useful phrases (3 minutes)

Learn these phrases and then test yourself.

Je voudrais vous inviter à dîner. *juh voodray voo zañveetay ah deenay*	I'd like to invite you for dinner.
Vous êtes libre mercredi prochain? *voo zet leebruh mairkrudee prochen*	Are you free next Wednesday?
Une autre fois peut-être. *oon awtruh fwah putetruh*	Another time perhaps.

Cultural tip When you go to someone's house for the first time, it is usual to bring flowers or wine. If you are invited again, having seen your host's house, you can bring something a little more personal.

3 In conversation (3 minutes)

Vous voulez venir dîner mardi?
voo voolay vuneer deenay mardee

Would you like to come to dinner on Tuesday?

Je suis désolée, je suis occupée.
juh swee dayzolay, juh swee zokoopay

I'm sorry, I'm busy.

Pourquoi pas jeudi?
poorkwah pah jurdee

What about Thursday?

4 **Words to remember** (3 minutes)

Familiarize yourself with these words and test yourself using the cover flap.

l'hôtesse (f)
lohtess
hostess

party	**la soirée** *lah swaray*
dinner party	**le dîner** *luh deenay*
invitation	**l'invitation** *lañveetasyoñ*
reception	**la réception** *lah raysepsyoñ*
cocktail party	**le cocktail** *luh koktail*

5 **Put into practice** (5 minutes)

Join in this conversation.

Vous pouvez venir à une réception ce soir.
voo poovay vuneer ah oon raysepsyoñ suh swah

Can you come to a reception this evening?

Say: Yes, I'd love to.

Oui, avec plaisir.
wee, avek playzeer

Merci de nous avoir invités.
mairsee duh noo zavwar añveetay
Thank you for inviting us.

Ça commence à huit heures.
sah komoñs ah weet ur

It starts at eight o'clock.

Ask: Should I dress formally?

Il faut s'habiller?
eel foe sabeeyay

Avec plaisir.
avek playzeer

I'd love to.

Venez avec votre mari.
vunay avek votruh maree

Please bring your husband.

Merci. A quelle heure?
mairsee. ah kel ur

Thank you. What time?

RÉVISEZ ET RÉPÉTEZ
Review and repeat

Réponses
Answers (Cover with flap)

1 Animals

❶ **le poisson**
luh pwassoñ

❷ **l'oiseau**
lwazoe

❸ **le lapin**
luh lapañ

❹ **le chat**
luh shah

❺ **le hamster**
luh amstair

❻ **le chien**
luh shiañ

1 Animals (3 minutes)

Say the French words for the numbered animals.

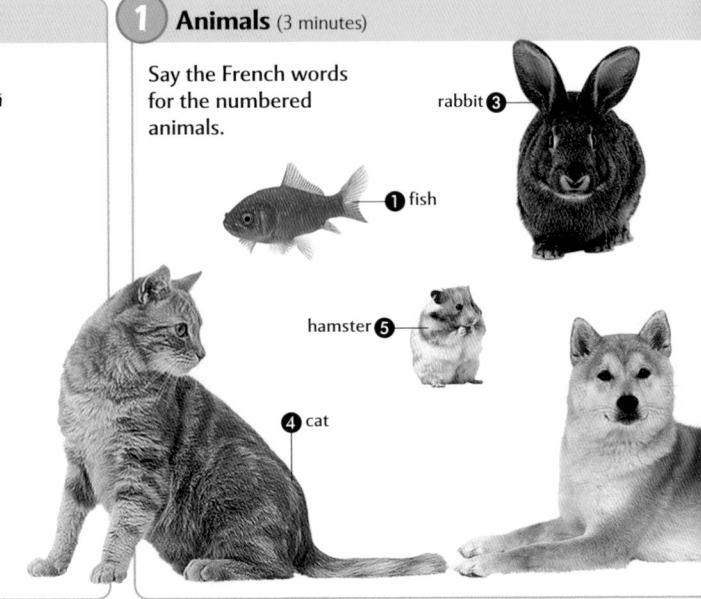

rabbit ❸

❶ fish

hamster ❺

❹ cat

2 I like...

❶ **J'aime le rugby.**
jem luh roogbee

❷ **Je n'aime pas le golf.**
juh nem pah luh golf

❸ **J'aime faire de la peinture.**
jem fair duh lah pañtyur

❹ **Je n'aime pas jouer aux boules.**
juh nem pah jooway oh bool

2 I like... (4 minutes)

Say the following in French.

❶ I like rugby.
❷ I don't like golf.
❸ I like painting.
❹ I don't like playing boules.

bird **2**

6 dog

3 To do (4 minutes)

Use the correct form of the verb **faire** in these sentences.

1 Tu _____ de la pêche?
2 Elle _____ de la voile.
3 Que _____ vous?
4 Il _____ froid aujourd'hui.
5 Vous _____ de la randonnée?
6 J'aime _____ de la natation.

3 To do

1 fais
fay
2 fait
fay
3 faites
fet
4 fait
fay
5 faites
fet
6 faire
fair

4 An invitation (4 minutes)

You are invited for dinner. Join in the conversation, replying in French following the English prompts.

Vous voulez venir pour déjeuner vendredi?
1 I'm sorry, I'm busy.

Pourquoi pas samedi?
2 I'd love to.

Venez avec vos enfants.
3 Thank you. At what time?

A douze heures et demie.
4 That's good for me.

4 An invitation

1 Je suis désolé(e),
je suis occupé(e).
*juh swee dayzolay,
juh swee zokoopay*

2 Avec plaisir.
avek playzeer

3 Merci. A quelle
heure?
mairsee, ah kel ur

4 C'est bon pour moi.
say boñ poor mwah

Reinforce and progress

Regular practice is the key to maintaining and advancing your language skills. In this section you will find a variety of suggestions for reinforcing and extending your knowledge of French. Many involve returning to exercises in the book and using the dictionaries to extend their scope. Go back through the lessons in a different order, mix and match activities to make up your own 15-minute daily program, or focus on topics that are of particular relevance to your current needs.

1 Warm up (1 minute)

Say "he is" and "they are." (pp.14-15)

Say "he is not" and "they are not." (pp.14-15)

What is French for "the children"? (pp.10-11)

Keep warmed up
Revisit the Warm Up boxes to remind yourself of key words and phrases. Make sure you work your way through all of them on a regular basis.

3 I'd like... (3 minutes)

Say you'd like the following:

bread ❸
jam ❷
❶ black coffee
large coffee ❹ with milk

Review and repeat again
Work through a Review and Repeat lesson as a way of reinforcing words and phrases presented in the course. Return to the main lesson for any topic on which you are no longer confident.

3 In conversation: taxi (2 minutes)

Carry on conversing
Reread the In Conversation panels. Say both parts of the conversation, paying attention to the pronunciation. Where possible, try incorporating new words from the dictionary.

Le marché aux fromages, s'il vous plaît.
luh marshayoe fromarj, seel voo play

The cheese market, please.

Oui, sans problème, monsieur.
wee. soñ problem musyuh

Yes, no problem, sir.

Vous pouvez me déposer ici, s'il vous plaît?
voo poovay muh dayposay eesee, seel voo play

Can you drop me

3 Useful phrases (5 minutes)

Familiarize yourself with these phrases and then test yourself.

The room is too cold/hot. **La chambre est trop froide/chaude.**
lah shombruh ay troe fwrard/shohd

Practice phrases
Return to the Useful Phrases and Put into Practice exercises. Test yourself using the cover flap. When you are confident, devise your own versions of the phrases, using new words from the dictionary.

There are no towels. **Il n'y a pas de serviettes.**
eenyah pah duh survyet

I need some soap. **J'ai besoin de savon.**
jay buzwañ duh savoñ

The shower doesn't work very well. **La douche ne marche pas très bien.**
lah doosh nuh marsh pah tray byañ

Match, repeat, and extend
Remind yourself of words related to specific topics by returning to the Match and Repeat and Words to Remember exercises. Test yourself using the cover flap. Discover new words in that area by referring to the dictionary and menu guide.

❷ lettuce

❸ lemons

❹ leeks

zucchini ❶

② Match and repeat (4 minutes)

Match the numbered items in this scene with the text in the panel.

❶ **les courgettes (f)**
lay korjet

❷ **la salade**
lah sah-lad

❸ **les citrons (m)**
lay sitroñ

❹ **les poireaux (m)**
lay pwaroe

❺ **les tomates (f)**
lay toemat

❻ **les champignons (m)**
lay shoñpeeyoñ

❼ **les avocats (m)**
lay zavokah

❽ **les pommes de terre (f)**
lay pom duh tair

tomatoes ❺

❻ mushrooms

potatoes ❽

avocados ❼

⑤ Say it (2 minutes)

Three kilos of potatoes, please.

The mushrooms are too expensive.

How much is the lettuce?

Say it again
The Say It exercises are a useful instant reminder for each lesson. Practice these, using your own vocabulary variations from the dictionary or elsewhere in the lesson.

Using other resources

In addition to working with this book, try the following language extension ideas:

Visit a French-speaking country and try out your new skills with native speakers. Find out if there is a French community near you. There may be stores, cafés, restaurants, and clubs. Try to visit some of these and use your French to order food and drink and strike up conversations. Most native speakers will be happy to speak French to you.

Join a language class or club. There are usually evening and day classes available at a variety of different levels. Or you could start a club yourself if you have friends who are also interested in keeping up their French.

Look at French magazines and newspapers. The pictures will help you to understand the text. Advertisements are also a useful way of expanding your vocabulary.

Use the Internet, where you can find all kinds of websites for learning languages, some of which offer free online help and activities. You can also find French websites for everything from renting a house to shampooing your pet. You can even access French radio and TV stations online. Start by going to a French search engine, such as *voila.fr*, and key in a subject that interests you, or set yourself a challenge: for example, finding a two-bedroom house for rent by the sea in Normandy.

MENU GUIDE

This guide lists the most common terms you may encounter on French menus or when shopping for food. If you can't find an exact phrase, try looking up its component parts.

A

abats *offal*
abricot *apricot*
à emporter *to go*
agneau *lamb*
aiguillette de bœuf
 slices of rump steak
ail *garlic*
ailloli *garlic mayonnaise*
à la broche *spit roast*
à la jardinière
 with assorted vegetables
à la normande *in cream sauce*
à la vapeur *steamed*
amande *almond*
ananas *pineapple*
anchois *anchovies*
andouillette *intestine sausage*
anguille *eel*
à point *medium*
artichaut *artichoke*
asperge *asparagus*
assiette anglaise
 selection of cold meats
au gratin *baked in a milk,*
 cream, and cheese sauce
au vin blanc *in white wine*
avocat *avocado*

B

banane *banana*
barbue *brill (fish)*
bavaroise *light mousse*
béarnaise *with béarnaise sauce*
bécasse *woodcock*
béchamel *white sauce*
beignet *fritter, doughnut*
beignet aux pommes *apple fritter*
betterave *beet*
beurre *butter*
beurre d'anchois *anchovy paste*
beurre noir *dark, melted butter*
bien cuit *well done*
bière *beer*
bière à la pression *draft beer*
bière blonde *lager*
bière brune *bitter beer*
bière panachée *beer with soda*
bifteck *steak*
bisque d'écrevisses *crayfish soup*

bisque de homard *lobster soup*
biscuit de Savoie *sponge cake*
blanquette de veau *veal stew*
bleu *very rare*
bleu d'auvergne
 blue cheese from Auvergne
bœuf bourguignon *beef*
 cooked in red wine
bœuf braisé *braised beef*
bœuf en daube *beef casserole*
bœuf miroton *beef and*
 onion stew
bœuf mode *beef stew*
 with carrots
bolet *boletus (mushroom)*
boudin blanc *white pudding*
boudin noir *black pudding*
bouillabaisse *fish soup*
bouilli *boiled*
bouillon *broth*
bouillon de légumes
 vegetable stock
bouillon de poule *chicken stock*
boulette *meatball*
bouquet rose *shrimp*
bourride *fish soup*
brandade *cod in cream and garlic*
brioche *round roll*
brochet *pike*
brochette *kebab*
brugnon *nectarine*
brûlot *flambéed brandy*
brut *very dry*

C

cabillaud *cod*
café *coffee (black)*
café au lait *coffee with milk*
café complet *continental*
 breakfast
café crème *coffee with milk*
café glacé *iced coffee*
café liégeois *iced coffee*
 with cream
caille *quail*
calamar/calmar *squid*
calvados *apple brandy*
canapé *small open*
 sandwich, canapé
canard *duck*
canard laqué *Peking duck*

caneton *duckling*
cantal *white cheese*
 from Auvergne
câpres *capers*
carbonnade *beef cooked in beer*
cari *curry*
carotte *carrot*
carottes Vichy *carrots*
 in butter and parsley
carpe *carp*
carré d'agneau *rack of lamb*
carrelet *plaice (fish)*
carte *menu*
carte des vins *wine list*
casse-croûte *snacks*
cassis *black currant*
cassoulet *bean, pork and*
 duck casserole
céleri/céleri rave *celeriac*
céleri en branches *celery*
cèpe *cep (mushroom)*
cerise *cherry*
cerises à l'eau de vie
 cherries in brandy
cervelle *brains*
chabichou *goat's and cow's*
 milk cheese
chablis *dry white wine from*
 Burgundy
champignon *mushroom*
champignon de Paris
 white button mushroom
chanterelle
 chanterelle (mushroom)
chantilly *whipped cream*
charcuterie *sausages, ham*
 and pâtés; pork products
charlotte *dessert with fruit,*
 cream, and cookies
chausson aux pommes
 apple turnover
cheval *horse*
chèvre *goat's cheese*
chevreuil *venison*
chicorée *endive*
chocolat chaud *hot chocolate*
chocolat glacé *iced chocolate*
chou *cabbage*
chou à la crème *cream puff*
choucroute *sauerkraut with*
 sausages and ham
chou-fleur *cauliflower*

chou rouge *red cabbage*
choux de Bruxelles
   Brussels sprouts
cidre *hard cider*
cidre doux *sweet cider*
citron *lemon*
citron pressé *fresh lemonade*
civet de lièvre *stewed hare*
clafoutis *baked batter*
   pudding with fruit
cochon de lait *suckling pig*
cocktail de crevettes
   shrimp cocktail
cœur *heart*
coing *quince*
colin *hake (fish)*
compote *stewed fruit*
comté *hard cheese from the Jura*
concombre *cucumber*
confit de canard
   duck preserved in fat
confit d'oie *goose preserved in fat*
confiture *jam*
congre *conger eel*
consommé *clear meat or*
   chicken soup
coq au vin *chicken in red wine*
coque *cockle*
coquelet *cockerel*
coquilles Saint-Jacques
   scallops in cream sauce
côte de porc *pork chop*
côtelette *chop*
cotriade bretonne *fish soup*
   from Brittany
coulommiers *rich, soft cheese*
court-bouillon *stock*
crabe *crab*
crème *cream; creamy sauce or*
   dessert; white (coffee)
crème à la vanille *vanilla custard*
crème anglaise *custard*
crème chantilly *whipped cream*
crème d'asperges *cream of*
   asparagus soup
crème de bolets *cream of*
   mushroom soup
crème de volaille *cream of*
   chicken soup
crème d'huîtres *cream*
   of oyster soup
crème fouettée *whipped cream*
crème pâtissière *rich, creamy*
   custard
crème renversée *set custard*
crème vichyssoise *cold leek*
   and potato soup
crêpe *crêpe*
crêpe à la crème de marron
   crêpe with chestnut cream
crêpe à l'œuf *crêpe with fried egg*
crêpe de froment *wheat crêpe*
crêpes Suzette *crêpes flambéed*
   with orange sauce

crépinette *small sausage patty*
   wrapped in fat
cresson *cress*
crevette grise *shrimp*
crevette rose *shrimp*
croque-madame *grilled cheese*
   and ham sandwich with a
   fried egg
croque-monsieur *grilled cheese*
   and ham sandwich
crottin de Chavignol
   small goat's cheese
crustacés *shellfish*
cuisses de grenouille
   frogs' legs

D

dartois *pastry with jam*
dégustation *wine-tasting*
digestif *liqueur*
dinde *turkey*
doux *sweet*

E

eau minérale gazeuse
   sparkling mineral water
eau minérale plate
   still mineral water
échalote *shallot*
écrevisse *freshwater crayfish*
endive *chicory*
en papillote *baked in foil*
   or paper
entrecôte *rib steak*
entrecôte au poivre
   peppered rib steak
entrecôte maître d'hôtel
   steak with butter and parsley
entrée *appetizer*
entremets *dessert*
épaule d'agneau farcie
   stuffed shoulder of lamb
épinards en branches
   leaf spinach
escalope de veau
   milanaise *veal escalope*
   with tomato sauce
escalope panée *breaded*
   escalope
escargot *snail*
estouffade de bœuf
   beef casserole
estragon *tarragon*

F

faisan *pheasant*
farci *stuffed*
fenouil *fennel*
filet *fillet*
filet de bœuf Rossini *fillet*
   of beef with foie gras

filet de perche *perch fillet*
fine *fine brandy*
flageolets *kidney beans*
flan *custard tart*
foie de veau *veal liver*
foie gras *goose or duck*
   liver preserve
foies de volaille *chicken livers*
fonds d'artichaut
   artichoke hearts
fondue bourguignonne
   meat fondue
fondue savoyarde
   cheese fondue
fraise *strawberry*
fraise des bois *wild strawberry*
framboise *raspberry*
frisée *curly lettuce*
frit *deep-fried*
frites *French fries*
fromage *cheese*
fromage blanc *cream cheese*
fromage de chèvre
   goat's cheese
fruits de mer *seafood*

G

galette *round, flat cake or savory*
   whole-wheat crêpe
garni *with potatoes and*
   vegetables
gâteau *cake*
gaufre *wafer; waffle*
gelée *gelatin*
Gewürztraminer *dry white*
   wine from Alsace
gibier *game*
gigot d'agneau *leg of lamb*
girolle *chanterelle (mushroom)*
glace *ice cream*
goujon *gudgeon (fish)*
gratin *dish baked with milk,*
   cheese, and cream
gratin dauphinois *sliced*
   potatoes baked in milk, cream,
   and cheese
gratinée *baked onion soup*
grillé *grilled*
grondin *gurnard (fish)*
groseille rouge *red currant*

H

hachis parmentier
   shepherd's pie
hareng mariné
   marinated herring
haricots *beans*
haricots blancs *haricot beans*
haricots verts *green beans*
homard *lobster*
hors-d'œuvre *appetizer*
huître *oyster*

I, J

îles flottantes *"floating islands"* *(soft meringue on custard)*
infusion *herb tea*
jambon *ham*
jambon de Bayonne *smoked and cured ham*
julienne *soup with chopped vegetables*
jus de fruits *fruit juice*
jus de pomme *apple juice*
jus d'orange *orange juice*

K, L

kir *white wine with black-currant liqueur*
kirsch *cherry brandy*
lait *milk*
laitue *lettuce*
langouste *saltwater crayfish*
langoustine *Dublin Bay prawn or Danish lobster*
lapereau *young rabbit*
lapin *rabbit*
lapin de garenne *wild rabbit*
lard *bacon*
légume *vegetable*
lentilles *lentils*
lièvre *hare*
limande *lemon sole*
livarot *strong, soft cheese from northern France*
longe *loin*
lotte *monkfish*
loup au fenouil *bass with fennel*

M

macédoine de légumes *mixed vegetables*
mache *corn salad (leafy vegetable)*
mangue *mango*
maquereau *mackerel*
marc *grape brandy*
marcassin *young boar*
marchand de vin *in red wine sauce*
marron *chestnut*
massepain *marzipan*
menthe *peppermint*
menthe à l'eau *mint cordial with water*
menu du jour *today's menu*
menu gastronomique *gourmet menu*
menu touristique *tourist menu*
merlan *whiting (fish)*
millefeuille *custard pastry*
millésime *vintage*
morille *morel (mushroom)*
morue *cod*

moules *mussels*
moules marinière *mussels in white wine*
mousseux *sparkling*
moutarde *mustard*
mouton *mutton*
mulet *mullet (fish)*
munster *strong cheese*
mûre *blackberry*
Muscadet *dry white wine*
myrtille *bilberry*

N

nature *plain*
navarin *mutton stew with vegetables*
navet *turnip*
noisette *hazelnut*
noisette d'agneau *medallion of lamb*
noix *nuts, walnuts*
nouilles *noodles*

O

œuf à la coque *boiled egg*
œuf dur *hard-boiled egg*
œuf mollet *soft-boiled egg*
œuf poché *poached egg*
œufs brouillés *scrambled eggs*
œuf sur le plat *fried egg*
oie *goose*
oignon *onion*
omelette au naturel *plain omelet*
omelette aux fines herbes *herb omelet*
omelette paysanne *omelet with potatoes and bacon*
orange pressée *fresh orange juice*
oseille *sorrel*
oursin *sea urchin*

P

pain *bread*
pain au chocolat *chocolate croissant*
palette de porc *shoulder of pork*
palourde *clam*
pamplemousse *grapefruit*
pastis *anise-flavored alcoholic drink*
pâté de canard *duck pâté*
pâté de foie de volaille *chicken liver pâté*
pâte feuilletée *puff pastry*
pâtes *pasta*
pêche *peach*
perdreau *young partridge*
perdrix *partridge*
petite friture *whitebait*

petit pain *roll*
petit pois *peas*
petits fours *small pastries*
petit suisse *cream cheese*
pied de porc *pig's feet*
pigeonneau *young pigeon*
pignatelle *cheese fritter*
pilaf de mouton *rice dish with mutton*
pintade *guinea fowl*
piperade *dish of egg, tomatoes, and peppers*
pissaladière *Provençal dish similar to pizza*
pistache *pistachio*
plat du jour *dish of the day*
plateau de fromages *cheese board*
pochouse *fish casserole with white wine*
poire *pear*
poireau *leek*
poisson *fish*
poivre *pepper*
poivron *red/green pepper*
pomme *apple*
pomme de terre *potato*
pommes de terre à l'anglaise *boiled potatoes*
pommes de terre en robe de chambre/des champs *baked potatoes*
pommes de terre sautées *fried potatoes*
pommes frites *French fries*
pommes paille *finely cut French fries*
pommes vapeur *steamed potatoes*
porc *pork*
potage *soup*
potage bilibi *fish and oyster soup*
potage Crécy *carrot and rice soup*
potage cressonnière *watercress soup*
potage Esaü *lentil soup*
potage parmentier *leek and potato soup*
potage printanier *vegetable soup*
potage Saint-Germain *split pea soup*
potage velouté *creamy soup*
pot-au-feu *beef and vegetable stew*
potée *vegetable and meat stew*
Pouilly-Fuissé *dry white wine from Burgundy*
poule au pot *chicken and vegetable stew*
poulet basquaise *chicken with ratatouille*

poulet chasseur *chicken with mushrooms and white wine*
poulet créole *chicken in white sauce with rice*
poulet rôti *roast chicken*
praire *clam*
provençale *with tomatoes, garlic and herbs*
prune *plum*
pruneau *prune*
pudding *plum pudding*
purée *mashed potatoes*

Q

quenelle *meat or fish dumpling*
queue de bœuf *oxtail*
quiche lorraine *egg, bacon, and cream quiche*

R

raclette *Swiss dish of melted cheese*
radis *radish*
ragoût *stew*
raie *skate* (**fish**)
raie au beurre noir *skate fried in butter*
raifort *horseradish*
raisin *grape*
râpé *grated*
rascasse *scorpion fish*
ratatouille *stew of peppers, zucchini, eggplant, and tomatoes*
ravigote *herb dressing*
reblochon *strong cheese from Savoy*
rémoulade *mayonnaise dressing with herbs, mustard, and capers*
rigotte *small goat's cheese from Lyon*
rillettes *preserved pork or goose meat*
ris de veau *veal sweetbread*
riz *rice*
riz pilaf *spicy rice with meat or seafood*
rognon *kidney*
roquefort *blue cheese*
rôti *roasted meat*
rouget *mullet*

S

sabayon *zabaglione (whipped egg yolk in Marsala wine)*
sablé *shortbread*
saignant *rare*
saint-honoré *cream puff cake*
saint-marcellin *goat's cheese*

salade composée *mixed salad*
salade russe *diced vegetables in mayonnaise*
salade verte *green salad*
salmis *game stew*
salsifis *oyster plant, salsify*
sanglier *wild boar*
sauce aurore *white sauce with tomato purée*
sauce béarnaise *thick sauce of eggs and butter*
sauce blanche *white sauce*
sauce gribiche *dressing with hard-boiled eggs*
sauce hollandaise *rich sauce of eggs, butter and vinegar, served with fish*
sauce Madère *Madeira sauce*
sauce matelote *wine sauce*
sauce Mornay *béchamel sauce with cheese*
sauce mousseline *hollandaise sauce with cream*
sauce poulette *sauce of mushrooms and egg yolks*
sauce ravigote *dressing with shallots and herbs*
sauce suprême *creamy sauce*
sauce tartare *mayonnaise with herbs and pickles*
sauce veloutée *white sauce with egg yolks and cream*
sauce vinot *wine sauce*
saucisse *sausage*
saucisse de Francfort *frankfurter*
saucisse de Strasbourg *beef sausage*
saucisson *salami*
saumon *salmon*
saumon fumé *smoked salmon*
sauternes *sweet white wine*
savarin *rum baba*
sec *dry*
seiche *cuttlefish*
sel *salt*
service (non) compris *service (not) included*
service 12% inclus *12% service charge included*
sole bonne femme *sole in white wine and mushrooms*
sole meunière *floured sole fried in butter*
soupe *soup*
soupe au pistou *thick vegetable soup with basil*
steak au poivre *peppered steak*
steak frites *steak and fries*
steak haché *ground beef*

steak tartare *raw ground beef with a raw egg*
sucre *sugar*
suprême de volaille *chicken in cream sauce*

T

tanche *tench (fish)*
tarte aux fraises *strawberry tart*
tarte aux pommes *apple tart*
tarte frangipane *almond cream tart*
tartelette *small tart*
tarte Tatin *baked apple dish*
tartine *bread and butter*
tendrons de veau *breast of veal*
terrine *pâté*
tête de veau *calf's head*
thé *tea*
thé à la menthe *mint tea*
thé au lait *tea with milk*
thé citron *lemon tea*
thon *tuna*
tomates farcies *stuffed tomatoes*
tome de Savoie *white cheese from Savoy*
tournedos *round beef steak*
tourte *covered pie*
tourteau *type of crab*
tripes à la mode de Caen *tripe in spicy vegetable sauce*
truite au bleu *poached trout*
truite aux amandes *trout with almonds*
truite meunière *trout in flour and fried in butter*

V, Y

vacherin *strong, soft cheese from the Jura*
vacherin glacé *ice cream meringue*
veau *veal*
velouté de tomate *cream of tomato soup*
vermicelle *vermicelli (very fine pasta)*
viande *meat*
vin *wine*
vinaigrette *oil and vinegar dressing*
vin blanc *white wine*
vin de pays *local wine*
vin de table *table wine*
vin rosé *rosé wine*
vin rouge *red wine*
volaille *poultry*
VSOP *mature brandy*
yaourt *yogurt*

DICTIONARY
English to French

The gender of a singular French noun is indicated by the word for *the*: **le** and **la** (masculine and feminine). If these are abbreviated to **l'** in front of a vowel or the letter *h*, or if the noun is plural, indicated by **les**, then the gender is indicated by the abbreviations (m) or (f). French adjectives (adj) vary according to the gender and number of the word they describe; the masculine form is shown here. In most cases, you add an **-e** to the masculine form to make it feminine. Certain endings use a different rule: masculine adjectives that end in **-x** adopt an **-se** ending in the feminine form, while those that end in **-ien** change to **-ienne**. Some feminine adjectives that do not follow these rules are shown here and follow the abbreviation (fem). For the plural form, a (silent) **-s** is usually added.

A

a **un/une**
about: about sixteen **environ seize**
accelerator **l'accélérateur** (m)
accident **l'accident** (m)
accommodation **l'hébergement** (m)
accountant **le/la comptable**
ache **la douleur**
adapter (plug) **la prise multiple;** (voltage) **l'adaptateur** (m)
address **l'adresse** (f)
adhesive **l'adhésif** (m)
admission charge **le prix d'entrée**
advance **l'avance** (f)
after **après**
afternoon **l'après-midi** (m)
aftershave **l'après-rasage** (m)
again **de nouveau**
against **contre**
agenda **l'ordre du jour** (m)
agent **l'agent** (m)
AIDS **SIDA**
air **l'air** (m)
air conditioning **la climatisation**
aircraft **l'avion** (m)
airline **la compagnie aérienne**
air mail **par avion**
air mattress **le matelas pneumatique**
airport **l'aéroport** (m)
airport bus **la navette (pour l'aéroport)**
aisle (supermarket) **rayon**
alarm clock **le réveil**
alcohol **l'alcool** (m)
Algeria **l'Algérie** (f)
Algerian **algérien(ne)**
all **tout;** *all the streets* **toutes les rues;** *that's all* **c'est tout**
allergic **allergique**
almost **presque**
alone **seul**
Alps **les Alpes** (f)
already **déjà**
always **toujours**
am: I am **je suis**
ambulance **l'ambulance** (f)
America **l'Amérique** (f)
American **américain(e)**
and **et**
Andorra **Andorre**
ankle **la cheville**
another (different) **un/une autre;** *another coffee, please* **encore un café, s'il vous plaît**
answering machine **le réponder**
antifreeze **l'antigel** (m)
antique shop **le magasin d'antiquités; l'antiquaire** (m)
antiseptic **l'antiseptique** (m)
apartment **l'appartement** (m)
aperitif **l'apéritif** (m)
appetite **l'appétit** (m)
appetizers **les entrées** (f)
apple **la pomme**
application form **le formulaire de demande**
appointment **le rendez-vous**
apricot **l'abricot** (m)
April **avril**
architecture **l'architecture** (f)
are: you are (singular informal) **tu es;** *we are* **nous sommes;** (plural; singular formal) **vous êtes;** *they are* **ils/elles sont**

arm **le bras**
armchair **le fauteuil**
arrival **l'arrivée** (f)
arrive **arriver**
art **l'art** (m)
art gallery **le musée d'art; la galerie d'art**
artist **l'artiste** (m)
as: as soon as possible **dès que possible**
ashtray **le cendrier**
asleep **endormi;** *he's asleep* **il dort**
aspirin **l'aspirine** (f)
associate professor **le maître de conférences**
asthmatic **asthmatique**
at: at the post office **à la poste;** *at the café* **au café;** *at 3 o'clock* **à 3 heures**
ATM **le distributeur automatique**
attic **le grenier**
attractive **attirant**
August **août**
aunt **la tante**
Australia **l'Australie** (f)
Australian **australien(ne)**
automatic **automatique**
autumn **l'automne** (m)
avocado **l'avocat** (m)
away: is it far away? **est-ce que c'est loin?;** *go away!* **allez-vous en!**
awful **affreux**
ax **la hache**
axle **l'essieu** (m)

B

baby **le bébé**
baby carriage **le landau**
baby wipes **les lingettes** (f)

back (not front) l'arrière (m);
(body) le dos; *I'll come back
tomorrow* je reviendrai
demain
backpack le sac à dos
bacon le bacon; *bacon and
eggs* des œufs au bacon
bad mauvais
baggage les bagages (m)
baggage check-in
l'enregistrement des
bagages (m)
baggage claim la
réclamation de bagages
bait l'appât (m)
bake cuire
bakery la pâtisserie
balcony le balcon
bald chauve
ball (soccer, etc.) le ballon;
(tennis, etc.) la balle
ballpoint pen le stylo-bille
banana la banane
band (musicians) le groupe
bandage le pansement, le
bandage
bangs (hair) la frange
bank la banque
bank note le billet
bar le bar;
barbecue le barbecue
barber's le coiffeur
bargain la affaire
basement le sous-sol
basin (sink) le lavabo
basket le panier
bath le bain; (bathtub) la
baignoire; *to take a bath*
prendre un bain
bathroom la salle de bains
battery (car) la batterie;
(flashlight) la pile
be être
beach la plage
beans les haricots (m)
beard la barbe
beautiful beau, (fem) belle
because parce que
bed le lit
bed linen les draps (m)
bedroom la chambre
beef le bœuf
beer la bière
before avant
beginner le débutant, la
débutante
beginners' slope la piste pour
débutants
behind derrière
beige beige
Belgian belge

Belgium la Belgique
bell (church) la cloche; (door)
la sonnette
below ... sous ...
belt la ceinture
beside à côté de
best: *the best* le meilleur
better mieux
between ... entre ...
bicycle la bicyclette, le vélo
big grand
bill l'addition (f)
bird l'oiseau (m)
birthday l'anniversaire (m);
happy birthday! joyeux
anniversaire!
bite (by dog) la morsure;
(by snake, insect) la piqûre;
(verb: dog) mordre; (insect,
snake) piquer
bitter amer
black noir
blackberry la mûre
black currant le cassis
blanket la couverture
bleach l'eau de Javel (f);
(verb) décolorer
blind (cannot see) aveugle;
(window) le store
blister l'ampoule (f)
blizzard la tempête de
neige
blond (adj) blond
blood le sang
blood test la prise de sang
blouse le chemisier
blue bleu
boarding pass la carte
d'embarquement
boat le bateau; (smaller)
la barque
body le corps
boil (verb) bouillir
boiled bouilli
boiler le chauffe-eau
bolt (on door) le verrou;
verrouiller (verb)
bone l'os (m); (fish) l'arête (f)
book le livre; réserver (verb)
bookstore la librairie
boot (footwear) la botte
border la frontière
boring ennuyeux
born: *I was born in ...* je suis
né(e) en ...
both les deux; *both of them*
tous les deux; *both of us*
nous deux; *both large and
small* grand et petit à la
fois
bottle la bouteille

bottle opener le décapsuleur,
l'ouvre-bouteille (m)
bottom le fond; (part of body)
le derrière
bowl le bol; (animal)
la gamelle
box la boîte
box office (theater, etc.)
le bureau de location
boy le garçon
boyfriend le petit ami
bra le soutien-gorge
bracelet le bracelet
brake le frein; (verb) freiner
branch la branche
brandy le cognac
bread le pain
bread shop la boulangerie
breakdown (car) la panne;
(nervous) la dépression;
My car has broken down (car)
je suis tombé en panne
breakfast le petit déjeuner
breathe respirer
bricklayer le maçon
bridge le pont
briefcase l'attaché-case (m)
British britannique
Brittany la Bretagne
brochure la brochure
broken cassé; *broken leg*
la jambe cassée; *broken
down* en panne
brooch la broche
brother le frère
brown marron
bruise le bleu
brush la brosse; (paintbrush)
le pinceau; (broom) le
balai; (verb) brosser
Brussels Bruxelles
bucket le seau
budget le budget
builder le constructeur
building le bâtiment
bumper le pare-chocs
bunker le bunker
burglary le cambriolage
burn la brûlure;(verb) brûler
bus le bus
business les affaires (f); *it's
none of your business* cela
ne vous regarde pas
business card la carte de
visite
bus station la gare routière
bus stop l'arrêt de bus (m)
busy (occupied) occupé;
(street) animé
but mais
butcher's la boucherie

butter **le beurre**
button **le bouton**
buy **acheter**
by: by the window **près de la fenêtre;** *by Friday* **d'ici vendredi;** *by myself* **tout seul;** *written by* **écrit par**

C

cabbage **le chou**
cabinet **le placard**
cable car **le téléphérique**
cable TV **la télé cablée**
café **le café**
cage **la cage**
cake **le gâteau**
calculator **la calculette**
call: what's it called? **comment est-ce que ça s'appelle?**
camcorder **le caméscope**
camera **l'appareil-photo** (m)
camper van **le camping-car**
campfire **le feu de camp**
campground **le terrain de camping**
campsite **l'emplacement** (m)
cam shaft **l'arbre à cames** (m)
can (vessel) **la boîte de conserve;** (to be able) **pouvoir;** *can I have ...?* **Je peux avoir ...?;** *can you ...?* **Vous pouvez ...?**
Canada **le Canada**
Canadian **canadien(ne)**
canal **le canal**
candle **la bougie**
canoe **le canoë**
can opener **l'ouvre-boîte** (m)
candy **le bonbon**
cap (hat) **la casquette;** (bottle) **la capsule**
car **la voiture;** (train) **la voiture, le wagon**
caravan **la caravane**
carburetor **le carburateur**
card **la carte**
careful **prudent;** *careful!* **attention!;** *be careful!* **soyez prudent!**
caretaker **le/la concierge**
carpenter **le charpentier**
carpet **le tapis**
carrot **la carotte**
car seat (for a baby) **le siège pour bébé**
cart **le chariot**
case **la valise**
cash **l'argent** (m); *to pay cash* **payer en liquide**

cashier **le guichet**
cassette **la cassette**
cassette player **le lecteur de cassettes**
castle **le château**
cat **le chat**
cathedral **la cathédrale**
cauliflower **le chou-fleur**
cave **la grotte**
CD **le disque compact**
ceiling **le plafond**
cell phone **le téléphone portable**
cellar **la cave**
cemetery **le cimetière**
center **le centre**
central heating **le chauffage central**
certificate **le certificat**
chair **la chaise**
change (money) **la monnaie;** (verb: money) **changer;** (clothes) **se changer**
Channel **la Manche**
Channel Islands **les îles Anglo-Normandes**
Channel Tunnel **le tunnel sous la Manche**
charger **le chargeur**
cheap **bon marché, pas cher**
check-in **l'enregistrement** (m)
check in **faire enregistrer ses bagages**
checkout (supermarket) **la caisse**
cheers! (toast) **santé!**
cheese **le fromage**
cheese shop **la fromagerie**
check **le chèque**
checkbook **le carnet de chèques**
cherry **la cerise**
chess **les échecs** (m)
chest **la poitrine**
chest of drawers **la commode**
chicken **le poulet**
child **l'enfant** (m)
children **les enfants** (m)
children's ward **le service de pédiatrie**
chimney **la cheminée**
china **la porcelaine**
chips **les chips** (f)
chocolate **le chocolat;** *a box of chocolates* **la boîte de chocolats;** *chocolate bar* **la tablette de chocolat**
chop (food) **la côtelette;** **couper** (verb: cut)

church **l'église** (f)
cigar **le cigare**
cigarette **la cigarette**
city **la ville**
class **la classe**
classical music **la musique classique**
clean (adj) **propre**
cleaner **la femme de ménages**
clear **clair**
clock **l'horloge** (f), **la pendule**
close **près** (near); **étouffant** (stuffy); **fermer** (verb)
closed **fermé**
clothes **les vêtements** (m)
clubs (cards) **trèfle**
clutch **l'embrayage** (m)
coat **le manteau**
coat hanger **le cintre**
cockroach **le cafard**
cocktail party **le cocktail**
coffee **le café;** *coffee with milk* **café crème**
coin **la pièce**
cold (illness) **le rhume;** **froid** (adj)
collar **le col, le collier**
collection (stamps, etc.) **la collection;**
color **la couleur**
color film **la pellicule couleur**
comb **le peigne;** **peigner** (verb)
come **venir;** *I come from ...* **je viens de ...;** *we came last week* **nous sommes arrivés la semaine dernière**
comforter **la couette**
company **la compagnie**
compartment **le compartiment**
complicated **compliqué**
computer **l'ordinateur** (m)
computer games **les jeux vidéos** (m)
concert **le concert**
conditioner (hair) **le baume après-shampooing**
condom **le préservatif**
conductor (orchestra) **le chef d'orchestre**
confectioner **le confiseur**
conference **la conférence**
conference room **la salle de conférences**
congratulations! **félicitations!**

consulate **le consulat**
consultant **consultant(e)**
contact lenses **les verres
de contact** (f)
contraceptive **le contraceptif**
cook **le cuisinier; faire
la cuisine** (verb)
cookie **le biscuit**
cooking utensils **les ut
ensiles de cuisine** (f)
cool **frais,** (fem) **fraîche**
cork **le bouchon**
corkscrew **le tire-bouchon**
corner **le coin**
corridor **le couloir**
Corsica **la Corse**
Corsican **corse**
cosmetics **les produits
de beauté** (m)
cost (verb) **coûter;**
how much does it
cost? **combien
ça coûte?**
cotton **le coton**
cotton balls **le coton
hydrophile**
cough **la toux; tousser** (verb)
countertop **le plan
de travail**
country (state) **le pays;** (not
town) **la campagne**
cousin **le cousin**
crab **le crabe**
cramp **la crampe**
crayfish (freshwater)
l'écrevisse (f); (saltwater)
la langouste
cream **la crème**
credit card **la carte
de crédit**
crêpe **la crêpe**
crib **le lit d'enfant**
cross (verb) **traverser**
crowded **bondé**
cruise **la croisière**
crutches **les béquilles** (f)
cry (weep) **pleurer;**
(shout) **crier**
cucumber **le concombre**
cufflinks **les boutons
de manchette** (m)
cup **la tasse**
curlers **les rouleaux** (m)
curls **les boucles** (f)
current **le courant**
curry **le curry**
curtain **le rideau**
customs **la douane**
cut **la coupure;** (verb)
couper
cycling **le vélo**

D

dad **papa**
dairy products **les produits
laitiers** (m)
dance **la danse;**(verb) **danser**
dangerous **dangereux**
dark **foncé;** dark blue
bleu foncé
daughter **la fille**
day **le jour**
dead **mort**
deaf **sourd**
dear **cher**
debit card **la carte bancaire**
December **décembre**
deck of cards **le jeu de cartes**
decorator **le décorateur**
deep **profond**
delay **le retard**
deliberately **exprès**
delicatessen **la charcuterie**
delivery **la livraison**
dentist **le/la dentiste**
dentures **le dentier**
deny **nier**
deodorant **le déodorant**
department **la département**
department store **le grand
magasin**
departures (airport, etc.)
le départ
designer **le designer**
desk **le bureau**
desserts **les desserts** (m)
develop **développer**
diabetic **diabétique**
diamond (jewel) **le diamant**
diamonds (cards) **carreau**
diaper **la couche**
diarrhea **la diarrhée**
dictionary **le dictionnaire**
die **mourir**
diesel **le diesel; le gazoile**
different **différent;**
that's different **c'est
différent;** I'd like a
different one **j'en voudrais
un autre**
difficult **difficile**
dining room **la salle
à manger**
dinner **le dîner**
dinner party **le dîner**
directory (telephone)
l'annuaire (m); **les
reseignments** (m)
disabled **handicapé**
disco **le discothèque**
discount **la réduction**
dish cloth **le torchon**

dishwasher **le lave-vaisselle**
dishwashing liquid **le produit
pour la vaisselle**
disposable diapers **les
couches à jeter** (f)
distributor (car) **le delco**
dive (verb) **plonger**
diving board **le plongeoir**
divorced **divorcé**
do **faire;** how do you do?
comment allez-vous?
dock **le quai**
doctor **le docteur; médecin**
document **le document**
dog **le chien**
doll **la poupée**
dollar **le dollar**
door (building) **la porte;** (car)
la portière
double room **la chambre
pour deux personnes**
doughnut **le beignet**
down **en bas**
downtown **le centre-ville**
drawer **le tiroir**
dress **la robe**
drink **la boisson;** (verb)
boire; would you like a
drink? **vous voulez boire
quelque chose?**
drinking water
l'eau potable (f)
drive (verb: car) **conduire**
driver **le conducteur**
driveway **le passage**
driver's license **le permis
de conduire**
drops **les goutes** (f)
drunk **soûl, ivre**
dry **sec,** (fem) **sèche**
dry-cleaner **le pressing**
during **pendant**
duster **le chiffon
à poussière**
duty-free **hors-taxe**

E

each (every) **chaque;**
two euros each
deux euros pièce
ear **l'oreille** (f)
early **tôt**
earrings **les boucles
d'oreille** (f)
east **l'est** (m)
easy **facile**
eat **manger**
egg **l'œuf** (m)
eight **huit**
eighteen **dix-huit**

eighty **quatre-vingt**
either: either of them
   n'importe lequel; *either ...*
   or ... **soit ... soit ...**
elastic **élastique**
elastic band **l'élastique** (m)
elbow **le coude**
electric **électrique**
electrician **électricien(ne)**
electricity **l'électricité** (f)
elevator **l'ascenseur** (m)
eleven **onze**
else: something else **autre**
   chose; *someone else*
   quelqu'un d'autre;
   somewhere else **ailleurs**
email **l'email** (m),
   le message,
   la messagerie
   électronique
email address **l'adresse**
   électronique (f)
embarrassing **gênant**
embassy **l'ambassade** (f)
embroidery **la broderie**
emerald **l'émeraude** (f)
emergency **l'urgence** (f)
emergency exit **la sortie**
   de secours
emergency room
   la salle des urgences
empty **vide**
end **la fin**
engaged (couple) **fiancé**
engine (car) **le moteur;** (train)
   la locomotive
engineer **l'ingénieur** (m)
engineering **l'ingénierie** (f)
England **l'Angleterre** (f)
English **anglais(e)**
enlargement
   l'agrandissement (m)
enough **assez**
entertainment
   le divertissement
entrance **l'entrée** (f)
envelope **l'enveloppe** (f)
epileptic **épileptique**
eraser **la gomme**
escalator **l'escalier**
   roulant (m)
especially **particulièrement**
estimate **l'estimation** (f)
evening **le soir**
every **chaque**
everyone **tout le monde**
everything **tout**
everywhere **partout**
example **l'exemple** (m); *for*
   example **par exemple**
excellent **excellent**

excess baggage **l'excédent**
   de bagages (m)
exchange (verb) **échanger**
exchange rate **le taux**
   de change
excursion **l'excursion** (f)
excuse me! **pardon!**
executive (in company)
   cadre (m)
exhaust (car) **le pot**
   d'echappement
exhibition **l'exposition** (f)
exit **la sortie**
expensive **cher**
extension lead **la rallonge**
exterior **l'extérieur** (m);
   extérieure (adj)
eye **l'œil** (m)
eyebrow **le sourcil**
eyes **les yeux** (m)

F
....

face **le visage**
faint **vague;** *to faint* **evanouir**
fair **la foire;** *(just)* **juste;** *it's*
   not fair **ce n'est pas juste**
fan (ventilator) **le**
   ventilateur; (enthusiast)
   le/la fan
fan belt **la courroie du**
   ventilateur
fantastic **fantastique**
far **loin;** *how far is it to ...?*
   est-ce que ...
   est loin d'ici?
fare **le prix du billet**
farm **la ferme**
farmer **le fermier**
fashion **la mode**
fast **rapide**
fat (of person) **gros,** (fem)
   grosse; (on meat, etc.)
   le gras
father **le père**
February **fevrier**
feel (touch) **toucher;**
   I feel hot **j'ai chaud;**
   I feel like ... **j'ai envie de ...;**
   I don't feel well **je ne me**
   sens pas bien
feet **les pieds** (m)
felt-tip pen **le feutre**
ferry (small) **le bac;** (large)
   le ferry
fever **la fièvre**
fiancé **le fiancé**
fiancée **la fiancée**
field **le champ;** (academic)
   secteur (m)
fifteen **quinze**

fifty **cinquante**
fig **la figue**
figures **les chiffres** (m)
filling (in tooth) **le plombage;**
   (in sandwich, cake)
   la garniture
film **le film**
filter paper **le papier filtre**
finger **le doigt**
fire **le feu;** (blaze)
   l'incendie (m)
fire extinguisher
   l'extincteur (m)
fireplace **la cheminée**
fireworks **le feu d'artifice**
first **premier**
first aid **les premiers**
   soins (m)
first class **première classe**
first floor **le premier étage**
first name **le prénom**
fish **le poisson**
fishing **la pêche;** *to go fishing*
   aller à la pêche
fishing rod **la canne à pêche**
fishmonger **la poissonnerie**
five **cinq**
flag **le drapeau**
flash (camera) **le flash**
flashlight **la lampe de poche**
flat (level) **plat**
flat tire **le pneu crevé**
flavor **le goût**
flea **la puce**
flight **le vol**
flight attendant
   l'hôtesse de l'air (f)
flip-flops **les tongs** (f)
flippers **les palmes** (f)
floor (ground) **le plancher;**
   (storey) **l'étage** (m)
florist **la fleuriste**
flour **la farine**
flower **la fleur**
flowerbed **le parterre**
   de fleurs
flute **la flûte**
fly (insect) **la mouche;** (verb:
   of plane, etc.) **voler;** (of
   person) **prendre l'avion**
fog **le brouillard**
folk music **la musique**
   folklorique
food **la nourriture**
food poisoning **l'intoxication**
   alimentaire (f)
foot **le pied**
for **pour;** *for me* **pour moi;**
   what for? **pour quoi faire?;**
   for a week **pour une**
   semaine

foreigner **l'étranger** (m)
forest **la forêt**
forget **oublier**
fork **la fourchette**
forty **quarante**
fountain pen **le stylo-plume**
four **quatre**
fourteen **quatorze**
fourth **quatrième**
France **la France**
free (no cost) **gratuit**; (at liberty) **libre**
freezer **le congélateur**
French **français(e)**
French fries **les frites** (f)
Friday **vendredi**
fried **frit**
friend **l'ami(e)**
friendly **amical, gentil**
front: in front **devant**
frost **le gel**
frozen foods **les produits surgelés** (m)
fruit **le fruit**
fruit juice **le jus de fruit**
fry **frire**
frying pan **la poêle**
full **complet**; *I'm full!* **j'ai l'estomac bien rempli!**
full board **la pension complète**
funny **drôle**
furnished **meublé**
furniture **les meubles** (m)

G

garage **le garage**
garbage **les ordures** (f); **les détritus** (m)
garbage can **la poubelle**
garden **le jardin**
garden center **la jardinerie**
garlic **l'ail** (m)
gas **le gaz**
gas-permeable lenses **les lentilles semi-souples** (f)
gas station **la station-service**
gasoline **l'essence** (f)
gate **le portail, la grille**; (at airport) **la porte d'embarquement**
gay **homosexuel**
gear (car) **la vitesse**
gearbox **la boîte de vitesses**
gearshift **le levier de vitesse**
gel **le gel**
German **allemand(e)**
Germany **l'Allemagne** (f)
get (fetch) **aller chercher**; *do you have ...?* **avez-vous ...?**;

to take the train **prendre le train**; *get back: we get back tomorrow* **nous rentrons demain**; *to get something back* **récupérer quelque chose**
get in **entrer**; (arrive) **arriver**
get off (bus, etc.) **descendre**
get on (bus, etc.) **monter**
get out **sortir**
get up **se lever**
gift **le cadeau**
gin **le gin**
ginger **le gingembre**
girl (child) **la fille**; (young woman) **la jeune fille**
girlfriend **la petite amie**
give **donner**
glad **heureux**
glass **le verre**
glasses **les lunettes** (f)
gloves **les gants** (m)
glue **la colle**
go **aller**
gold **l'or** (m)
golf **le golf**
golf course **le parcours de golf**
good **bon**, (fem) **bonne**; *good!* **bien!**
goodbye **au revoir**
good evening **bonsoir**
government **le gouvernement**
granddaughter **la petite-fille**
grandfather **le grand-père**
grandmother **la grand-mère**
grandparents **les grands-parents** (m)
grandson **le petit-fils**
grapes **les raisins** (m)
grass **l'herbe** (f)
gray **gris**
Great Britain **la Grande-Bretagne**
green **vert**
grill **le gril**
grilled **grillé(e)**
grocery store **l'épicerie** (f)
ground floor **le rez-de-chaussée**
groundsheet **le tapis de sol**
guarantee **la garantie**; (verb) **garantir**
guard (train) **le chef de train**
guest **l'invitée**
guide **le/la guide**
guide book **le guide**
guitar **la guitare**
gun (rifle) **le fusil**; (pistol) **le pistolet**
gutter **la gouttière**
gym **le centre sportif**

H

hair **les cheveux** (m); *long/short hair* **les chevaux longs/courts**
haircut **la coupe** (de cheveux)
hairdresser **le coiffeur**
hairdryer **le sèche-cheveux**
hairspray **la laque**
half **demi**; *half an hour* **une demi-heure**
half-board **la demi-pension**
ham **le jambon**
hamburger **le hamburger**
hammer **le marteau**
hamster **le hamster**
hand **la main**
hand luggage **le bagage à main**
handbag **le sac à main**
handbrake **le frein à main**
handkerchief **le mouchoir**
handle (door) **la poignée**
handsome **beau**
hangover **la gueule de bois**
happy **heureux**
harbor **le port**
hard **dur**; (difficult) **difficile**
hard lenses **les lentilles rigides** (f)
hardware store **la quincaillerie**
hat **le chapeau**
have **avoir**; *do you have ...?* **avez-vous ...?**
hay fever **le rhume des foins**
he **il**
head **la tête**
headache **le mal à la tête**
headlights **les phares** (m)
headphones **les écouteurs** (m)
headquarters **le siège social**
hear **entendre**
hearing aid **l'appareil acoustique**
heart **le cœur**
heart condition **le problème au cœur**
hearts (cards) **cœurs**
heater **le radiateur**
heating **le chauffage**
heavy **lourd**
hedge **la haie**
heel **le talon**
hello **bonjour**
help **l'aide** (f); (verb) **aider**
hepatitis **l'hépatite** (f)
her: it's for her **c'est pour elle**; *give it to her* **donnez-le lui**
her: her book **son livre**; *her*

house sa maison; *her shoes* ses chaussures; *it's hers* c'est à elle
hi salut
high haut
highway l'autoroute (f)
highway code le code de la route
hiking la randonée
hill la colline
him: it's for him c'est pour lui; *give it to him* donnez-le lui
his: his book son livre; *his house* sa maison; *his shoes* ses chaussures; *it's his* c'est à lui
history l'histoire (f)
hitchhike faire de l'autostop
HIV-positive séropositif(ve)
hobby le passe-temps
home: at home (my home) chez moi; *he's at home* il est chez lui
homeopathy homéopathie
honest honnête
honey le miel
honeymoon la lune de miel
hood (car) le capot
horn (car) le klaxon; *(animal)* la corne
horrible horrible
hospital l'hôpital (m)
host l'hôte (m)
hostess l'hôtesse (f)
hot chaud
hotel l'hôtel (m)
hour l'heure (f)
house la maison
household products les produits entretien (m)
hovercraft l'aéroglisseur (m)
hoverport l'hoverport (m)
how? comment?
how much? combien?
hundred cent
hungry: I'm hungry j'ai faim
hurry: I'm in a hurry je suis pressé
husband le mari
hydrofoil l'hydrofoil (m)

I

I je
ice la glace
ice cream la glace
ice rink la patinoire
ice skates les patins à glace (m)
ice-skating: to go ice-skating aller patiner

identification la identification
if si
ignition l'allumage (m)
ill malade
immediately immédiatement
impossible impossible
in dans; *in France* en France
indigestion l'indigestion (f)
inexpensive bon marché, pas cher
infection l'infection (f)
information l'information (f)
injection la piqûre
injury la blessure
ink l'encre (f)
inn l'auberge (f)
inner tube la chambre à air
insect l'insecte (m)
insect repellent la crème anti-insecte
insomnia l'insomnie (f)
instant coffee le café soluble
insurance l'assurance (f)
interesting intéressant
Internet l'internet (m)
interpret interpréter
interpreter l'interprète (m)
invitation l'invitation (f)
invoice la facture
Ireland l'Irlande (f)
Irish irlandais(e)
iron ((for clothes) le fer à repasser; *(verb)* repasser
is: he/she is il/elle est; *it is* c'est
island l'île (f)
it il; elle
Italian italien(ne)
Italy l'Italie (f)
its son; sa; ses *(see his)*

J

jacket la veste
jam la confiture
January janvier
jazz le jazz
jeans les jeans (m)
jellyfish la méduse
jeweler la bijouterie
job le travail
jog (verb) faire du jogging; *to go for a jog* aller faire du jogging
jogging suit le survêtement
joke la plaisanterie
journey le voyage
July juillet
June juin

just: it's just arrived ça vient juste d'arriver; *I've just one left* il ne m'en reste qu'un

K

kerosene le pétrole
kettle la bouilloire
key la clé
keyboard le clavier
kidney le rein
kilo le kilo
kilometer le kilomètre
kind gentil
kitchen la cuisine
knee le genou
knife le couteau
knitting needle l'aiguille à tricoter (f)
know (fact) savoir; *(person)* connaître; *I don't know* je ne sais pas

L

label l'étiquette (f)
lace la dentelle; *(of shoe)* le lacet
lake le lac
lamb l'agneau (m)
lamp la lampe
lampshade l'abat-jour (m)
land la terre; *(verb)* atterrir
language la langue
laptop l'ordinateur portable (m)
large grand
last (final) dernier; *last week* la semaine dernière; *at last!* enfin!
last name le nom de famille
late tard; *the bus is late* le bus est en retard
later plus tard
laugh rire
laundromat la laverie automatique
laundry (place) la blanchisserie; *(clothes)* le linge
laundry detergent la lessive
law (subject) le droit
lawn la pelouse
lawnmower la tondeuse à gazon
lawyer avocat(e)
laxative le laxatif
lazy paresseux
lead la laisse
leaf la feuille

leaflet **le dépliant**
learn **apprendre**
leather **le cuir**
lecture hall **l'amphithéâtre** (m)
leek **le poireaux**
left (not right) **la gauche;** *there's nothing left* **il ne reste plus rien**
leg **la jambe**
lemon **le citron**
lemonade **le citron pressé**
length **la longueur**
lens (camera) **l'objectif** (m)
less **moins**
lesson **la leçon**
letter **la lettre**
lettuce **la salade**
library **la bibliothèque**
license **le permis**
license plate **la plaque d'immatriculation**
life **la vie**
light **la lumière;** (not heavy) **léger;** (not dark) **clair**
light bulb **l'ampoule** (f)
lighter **le briquet**
lighter fluid **le gaz à briquet**
light meter **la cellule photoélectrique**
like (verb) **aimer:** *I like swimming* **j'aime nager;** *I don't like* **je n'aime pas;** (similar to) **comme**
lime (fruit) **le citron vert**
lipstick **le rouge à lèvres**
liqueur **la liqueur**
list **la liste**
liter **le litre**
literature **la litérature**
litter **les ordures** (f)
little (small) **petit;** *it's a little big* **c'est un peu trop grand;** *just a little* **juste un peu**
liver **le foie**
living room **le salon**
lobster **le homard**
lollipop **la sucette**
long **long,** (fem) **longue**
lost property **les objets trouvés** (m)
loud **fort;** (color) **criard**
love **l'amour** (m); (verb) **aimer**
lover **l'amant** (m)
low **bas**
luck **la chance;** *good luck!* **bonne chance!**
luggage **les bagages** (m)
luggage lockers **la consigne automatique**

luggage rack **le porte-bagages**
lunch **le déjeuner**
Luxembourg **le Luxembourg**

M

mad **fou,** (fem) **folle**
magazine **la revue**
maid **la femme de chambre**
mail **la poste;** (verb) **poster**
mail carrier **le facteur**
mailbox **la boîte à lettres**
main courses **les plats** (m)
make **faire**
makeup **le maquillage**
man **l'homme** (m)
manager **le directeur; le chef**
many **beaucoup;** *not many* **pas beaucoup**
map **la carte;** (town map) **le plan**
March **mars**
margarine **la margarine**
market **le marché**
marmalade **la marmelade d'oranges**
married **marié**
mascara **le mascara**
mass (church) **la messe**
mast **le mât**
match (light) **l'allumette** (f); (sport) **le match**
material (cloth) **le tissu**
matter: *it doesn't matter* **ça ne fait rien**
mattress **le matelas**
May **mai**
maybe **peut-être**
me: *it's me* **c'est moi;** *it's for me* **c'est pour moi;** *give it to me* **donnez-le-moi**
meal **le repas**
mean: *what does this mean?* **qu'est-ce que cela veut dire?**
meat **la viande**
mechanic **le mécanicien, le garagiste**
medication **les médicaments** (m)
medicine **le médicament;** (subject) **le médicine**
Mediterranean **la Méditerranée**
meeting **la réunion**
melon **le melon**
menu **la carte;** *set menu* **le menu**
message **le message**

metro **le métro**
microwave **le micro-ondes**
middle **le milieu**
midnight **minuit**
milk **le lait**
mine: *it's mine* **c'est à moi**
mineral water **l'eau minérale** (f)
minute **la minute**
mirror **le miroir;** (car) **le rétroviseur**
Miss **Mademoiselle**
mistake **l'erreur** (f)
modem **le modem**
Monday **lundi**
money **l'argent** (m)
monitor (computer) **le moniteur**
month **le mois**
monument **le monument**
moon **la lune**
moped **la mobylette**
more **plus;** *more or less* **plus ou moins**
morning **le matin;** *in the morning* **dans la matinée**
mosquito **le moustique**
mother **la mère**
motorboat **le bateau à moteur**
motorcycle **la moto**
mountain **la montagne**
mountain bike **le vélo tout terrain**
mouse **la souris**
mousse (hair) **la mousse**
mouth **la bouche**
move **bouger;** (house) **déménager;** *don't move!* **ne bougez pas!**
movie theater **le cinéma**
Mr. **Monsieur**
Mrs. **Madame**
mug **la tasse**
museum **le musée**
mushroom **le champignon**
music **la musique**
musical instrument **l'instrument de musique** (m)
musician **le musicien**
mussels **les moules** (f)
must: *I must* **je dois**
mustache **la moustache**
mustard **la moutarde**
my: *my book* **mon livre;** *my house* **ma maison;** *my shoes* **mes chaussures**

N

nail (metal) **le clou;** (finger) **l'ongle** (m)
nail clippers **la pince à ongles**
nail file **la lime à ongles**
nail polish **le vernis à ongles**
name **le nom;** *what's your name* **comment vous appelez-vous?**
narrow **étroit**
near: near the door **près de la porte**
necessary **nécessaire**
neck **le cou**
necklace **le collier**
need (verb) **avoir besoin de;** *I need ...* **j'ai besoin de ...;** *there's no need* **ce n'est pas nécessaire**
needle **l'aiguille** (f)
negative (photo) **le négatif**
neither: neither of them **ni l'un ni l'autre;** *neither ... nor ...* **ni ... ni ...**
nephew **le neveu**
never **jamais**
new **nouveau,** (fem) **nouvelle; neuf,** (fem) **neuve**
news **les nouvelles** (f); (television) **les informations** (f)
newspaper **le journal**
newsstand **le tabac;** **le tabac-journaux**
next **prochain;** *next week* **la semaine prochaine;** *what next?* **et puis quoi?**
nice (place, etc.) **joli;** (person) **sympathique**
niece **la nièce**
night **la nuit**
nightclub **la boîte de nuit**
nightgown **la chemise de nuit**
nine **neuf**
nineteen **dix-neuf**
ninety **quatre-vingt-dix**
no (response) **non;** (not any) **aucun**
nobody **personne**
noisy **bruyant**
none **aucun**
noon **midday**
north **le nord**
nose **le nez**
not **pas;** *he's not ...* **il n'est pas ...**
notebook **le carnet**
notepad **le bloc notes**
nothing **rien**
novel **le roman**
November **novembre**
now **maintenant**
nowhere **nulle part**
nudist **le nudiste**
number (figure) **le numéro;** (amount) **le nombre**
nurse **infirmier;** (fem) **infirmière**
nut (fruit) **la noix;** (for bolt) **l'écrou** (m)

O

oars **les rames** (f)
occasionally **de temps en temps**
October **octobre**
of **de**
of course **bien sûr**
office **le bureau**
often **souvent**
oil **l'huile** (f)
ointment **la pommade**
OK **d'accord**
old **vieux,** (fem) **vieille;** *how old are you?* **quel âge avez-vous?**
olive **l'olive** (f)
omelet **l'omelette** (f)
on ... **sur ...**
one **un/une**
one-way ticket **l'aller simple** (m) *onion* **l'oignon** (m)
only **seulement**
open (adj) **ouvert;** (verb) **ouvrir**
opening times **les heures d'ouverture** (f)
operating room **la salle d'opérations**
operation **l'opération** (f)
operator (phone) **l'opérateur** (m)
opposite **en face de**
optician's **l'opticien** (m)
or **ou**
orange (fruit) **l'orange** (f); (color) **orange**
orange juice **le jus d'orange**
orchestra **l'orchestre** (m)
ordinary **habituel**
organ (music) **l'orgue** (m)
other: the other ... **l'autre ...**
our: our house **notre maison;** *our children* **nos enfants;** *it's ours* **c'est à nous**
out: he's out **il n'est pas là**
outside **dehors**

oven **le four**
over (above) **au-dessus de;** (more than) **plus de;** (finished) **fini;** *it's over the road* **c'est de l'autre côté de la rue;** *over there* **là-bas**
oyster **l'huître** (f)

P

package **le paquet;** (parcel) **le colis**
package **le colis**
packet **le paquet**
padlock **le cadenas**
page **la page**
pain **la douleur**
paint **la peinture**
painting **la peinture**
pair **la paire**
palace **le palais**
pale **pâle, blême**
pants **le pantalon**
panty hose **les collants** (m)
paper **le papier;** (newspaper) **le journal**
pardon? **pardon?**
parents **les parents** (m)
park **le jardin public;** (verb) **garer**
parking lot **le parking**
part (in hair) **la raie**
party (celebration) **la fête, la soirée;** (group) le **groupe;** (political) **le parti**
pass (in a car) **doubler**
passenger **le passager**
passport **le passeport**
passport control **le contrôle des passeports**
password **le mot de passe**
pasta **les pâtes** (f)
path **le chemin, l'allée** (f)
pay **payer**
payment **le paiement**
peach **la pêche**
peanuts **les cacahuètes** (f)
pear **la poire**
pearl **la perle**
peas **les petits pois** (m)
pedestrian **le piéton**
peg **la pince à linge**
pen **le stylo**
pencil **le crayon**
pencil sharpener **le taille-crayon**
penknife **le canif**
pen pal **le correspondant**
people **les gens** (m)
pepper (and salt) **le poivre;** (red/green) **le poivron**

peppermints les
bonbons à la
menthe (m)
per: per night par nuit
perfect parfait
perfume le parfum
perhaps peut-être
perm la permanente
pet passport le passeport
d'animaux
pets les animaux
(familiers) (m)
pharmacy la pharmacie
phone card la carte
téléphonique
photocopier le copieur
photograph la photo; (verb)
photographier
photographer le/la
photographe
phrasebook le guide
de conversation
piano le piano
pickpocket le pickpocket
pickup (mail) la levée
picnic le pique-nique
piece le morceau
pill le comprimé
pillow l'oreiller (m)
pilot le pilote
PIN le code
pin l'épingle (f)
pineapple l'ananas (m)
pink rose
pipe (for smoking) la pipe;
(for water) le tuyau
piston le piston
pizza la pizza
place l'endroit (m);
at your place
chez vous
planner l'agenda (m)
plant la plante
plaster le pansement
plastic le plastique
plastic bag le sac
plastic wrap le film
alimentaire
transparent
plate l'assiette (f)
platform le quai
play (theater) la pièce;
(verb) jouer
please s'il vous plaît
pleased: pleased to meet you
enchanté(e)
plug (electrical) la prise;
(sink) le bouchon
plumber (occupation)
le plombier
pocket la poche

poison le poison
police la police
police officer le policier
police report le rapport
de police
police station
le commissariat
politics la politique
poor pauvre;
(bad quality) mauvais
pop music la musique
pop
pork le porc
port (harbor) le port;
(drink) le porto
porter le porteur
possible possible
postal (ZIP) code
le code postal
postcard la carte
postale
poster (outside) l'affiche (f);
(inside) le poster
post office la poste
potato la pomme
de terre
poultry la volaille
pound (weight) la livre
powder la poudre
prefer préférer
prepared meals
les plats préparés (m)
prescription l'ordonnance (f)
pretty (beautiful) joli;
(quite) plutôt
price le prix
priest le prêtre
printer l'imprimante (f)
private privé
problem le problème
profession la profession
professor le professeur
profits les bénéfices (m)
public le public
pull tirer
puncture (tire) la crevaison
purple violet
purse le porte-monnaie
push pousser
put mettre
pyjamas le pyjama

Q

quality la qualité
quarter le quart
question la question
quick rapide
quiet (preson) silencieux;
(street, etc.) tranquille
quite (fairly) assez

R

rabbit le lapin
radiator le radiateur
radio la radio
radish le radis
rail: by rail par chemin
de fer
railroad le chemin de fer
rain la pluie
raincoat l'imperméable (m)
raisin le raisin sec
rake le râteau
rare (uncommon) rare;
(steak) saignant
rash la rougeur
raspberry la framboise
rat le rat
razor blades les lames
de rasoir (f)
read lire
reading lamp la lampe
de bureau; (bedside)
la lampe de chevet
ready prêt
receipt le reçu
reception la réception
receptionist le/la
receptionniste
record (music) le disque;
(sports, etc.) le record
record player
le tourne-disque
record store le disquaire
red rouge; (hair) roux
refreshments les
rafraîchissements (m)
refrigerator le frigo
registered mail en
recommandé
relax se détendre
religion la religion
remember: I remember je m'en
souviens; I don't remember
je ne me souviens pas
rent (verb) louer
reservation la réservation
reserve (verb) réserver
rest (remainder) le reste;
(verb: relax) se reposer
restaurant le restaurant
restaurant car
le wagon-restaurant
restrooms les toilettes (f)
return (come back) revenir;
(give back) rendre
rice le riz
rich riche
right (correct) juste; (not left)
la droite
ring (jewelry) la bague

ripe **mûr**
river **le fleuve**
road **la route**; (in town)
   la rue
roasted **rôti**
rock (stone) **le rocher**;
   (music) **le rock**
roll (bread) **le petit pain**
roof **le toit**
room **la chambre**; (space)
   la place
room service **le room service**
rope **la corde**
rose **la rose**
round (circular) **rond**; *it's my
   round* **c'est ma tournée**
   (buying drinks)
round-trip ticket
   l'aller retour (m)
roundabout **le rond-point**
row (verb) **ramer**
rowboat **la barque**
rubber (material)
   le caoutchouc
rug (mat) **la carpette**;
   (blanket) **la couverture**
rugby **le rugby**
ruins **les ruines** (f)
ruler **la règle**
rum **le rhum**
run (verb) **courir**
runway **la piste**

S

sad **triste**
safe (not in danger)
   en sécurité; (not
   dangerous) **sans danger**
safety pin **l'épingle de
   nourrice** (f)
sailing **la voile**
sailboat **le voilier**
salad **la salade**
sale **la vente**; (at reduced
   prices) **les soldes** (f)
salmon **le saumon**
salt **le sel**
same: the same ... **le/la
   même ...**; *the same again,
   please* **la même chose,
   s'il vous plaît**
sand **le sable**
sandals **les sandales** (f)
sand dunes **les dunes** (f)
sandwich **le sandwich**
sanitary napkins
   **les serviettes
   hygiéniques** (f)
Saturday **samedi**
sauce **la sauce**

saucer **la soucoupe**
saucepan **la casserole**
sauna **le sauna**
sausage **la saucisse**
say **dire**; *what did you say?*;
   qu'avez-vous dit?; *how do
   you say ...?* **comment
   dit-on ...?**
scarf **l'écharpe** (f); (head)
   le foulard
schedule **l'emploi du temps**
   (m); (train, bus) **l'horaire** (f)
school **l'école** (f)
science **la science**
scissors **les ciseaux** (m)
Scotland **l'Ecosse** (f)
screen **l'écran** (m)
screw **la vis**
screwdriver **le tournevis**
sea **la mer**
seafood **les fruits de mer** (m)
seat **la place**
seat belt **la ceinture
   de sécurité**
second (of time) **la seconde**;
   (in series) **deuxième**
second class **en seconde**
secretary **le/la secrétaire**
see **voir**; *I can't see* **je ne vois
   rien**; *I see* **je vois**
self-employed **à mon compte**
sell **vendre**
seminar **le séminaire**
send **envoyer**
separate (adj) **séparé**;
   (verb) **séparer**
September **septembre**
serious **sérieux**
seven **sept**
seventeen **dix-sept**
seventy **soixante-dix**
several **plusieurs**
sew **coudre**
shampoo **le shampooing**
shave: to shave **se raser**
shaving foam
   la mousse à raser
shawl **le châle**
she **elle**
sheet **le drap**
shell **la coquille**
shellfish **les crustacés** (m)
ship **le bateau**
shirt **la chemise**
shoelaces **les lacets** (m)
shoemaker **la cordonnerie**
shoe polish **le cirage**
shoes **les chaussures** (f)
shop **le magasin**
shopkeeper **commerçant**;
   (fem) **commerçante**

shopping **les courses** (f); *to
   go shopping* **faire les
   courses**
short **court**; **petit**
shorts **le short**
shoulder **l'épaule** (f)
shower (bath) **la douche**;
   (rain) **l'averse** (f)
shower gel **le gel douche**
shrimp **la crevette**
shutter (camera) **l'obturateur**
   (m); (window) **le volet**
sick: I feel sick **j'ai envie
   de vomir**; *to be sick*
   (vomit) **vomir**
side (edge) **le bord**
sidelights **les feux de
   position** (m)
sidewalk **le trottoir**
sightseeing **le tourism**
silk **la soie**
silver (color) **argenté**;
   (metal) **l'argent** (m)
simple **simple**
sing **chanter**
single (one) **seul**;
   (unmarried) **célibataire**
single room **la chambre pour
   une personne**; **la
   chambre simple**
sink **l'évier** (m)
sir **monsieur**
sister **la sœur**
six **six**
sixteen **seize**
sixty **soixante**
size **la taille**
skates **les patins à glace** (m)
ski **le ski**; (verb) **skier**
ski boots **les chaussures
   de ski** (f)
skid (verb) **déraper**
skiing: to go skiing **faire du ski**
ski lift **le remonte-pente**
skin cleanser **le démaquillant**
ski pole **le bâton de ski**
ski resort **la station de ski**
skirt **la jupe**
sky **le ciel**
sled **la luge**
sleep **le sommeil**;
   (verb) **dormir**
sleeper car **le wagon-lit**
sleeping bag **le sac de
   couchage**
sleeping pill **le somnifère**
sleeve **la manche**
slip **le jupon**
slippers **les pantoufles** (f)
slow **lent**
small **petit**

la rivière; (big) *smell*
  l'odeur (f);(verb) **sentir**
smart **intelligent**
smile **le sourire;**
  (verb) **sourire**
smoke **la fumée;**
  (verb) **fumer**
snack **le snack**
snow **la neige**
so **si**
soaking solution
  (for contact lenses)
  la solution de
  trempage
soap **le savon**
soccer **le football**
socks **les chaussettes** (f)
soft **mou**
soft lenses **les lentilles**
  souples (f)
soil **la terre**
somebody **quelqu'un**
somehow **d'une façon ou**
  d'une autre
something **quelque chose**
sometimes **quelquefois**
somewhere **quelque**
  part
son **le fils**
song **la chanson**
sorry (apology) **pardon;** *sorry?*
  (pardon?) **pardon?;** *I'm*
  sorry **je suis désolé**
soup **la soupe**
south **le sud**
souvenir **le souvenir**
spade (shovel) **la pelle;**
  (garden) **la bêche**
spades (cards) **pique**
Spain **l'Espagne** (f)
Spanish **espagnol**
spare parts **les pièces**
  de rechange (f)
spark plug **la bougie**
sparkling water
  l'eau gazeuse (f)
speak **parler;** *do you speak ...?*
  parlez-vous ...?; *I don't*
  speak ... **je ne parle pas ...**
speed **la vitesse**
speed limit **la limitation**
  de vitesse
spider **l'araignée** (f)
spinach **les épinards** (m)
spoon **la cuillère**
sport **le sport**
spring (mechanical)
  le ressort; (season)
  le printemps
square (in town) **la place;**
  (adj: shape) **carré**

stadium **le stade**
staircase **l'escalier** (m)
stairs **les escaliers** (m)
stamp **le timbre**
stand in line **faire la queue**
stapler **l'agrafeuse** (f)
star **l'étoile** (f); (movie)
  la vedette
start (beginning) **le début;**
  (verb) **commencer**
statement **la déposition**
station **la gare;** (metro)
  la station
statue **la statue**
steak **le steak**
steal **voler;** *it's been stolen*
  on l'a volé
steamed **à la vapeur**
steamer **le bateau à vapeur;**
  (cooking) **le couscoussier**
steering wheel **le volant**
sting **la piqûre;** (verb) **piquer**
stockings **les bas** (m)
stomach **l'estomac** (m)
stomachache **le mal**
  de ventre, le mal à
  l'estomac
stop (bus) **l'arrêt (de bus)**
  (m); (verb) **s'arrêter**
storm **la tempête**
stove **la cuisinière**
straight ahead **tout droit**
strawberry **la fraise**
stream (small river)
  le ruisseau
street **la rue**
street musician **le musicien**
  des rues
string (cord) **la ficelle;**
  (guitar, etc.) **la corde**
stroller **la poussette**
strong (person, drink) **fort;**
  (material) **résistant**
student **l'étudiant** (m)
stupid **stupide**
suburbs **la banlieue**
subway **le métro**
sugar **le sucre**
suit **le costume;** *it suits you*
  ça vous va bien
suitcase **la valise**
summer **l'été** (m)
sun **le soleil**
sunbathe **se faire bronzer**
sunburn **le coup de soleil**
Sunday **dimanche**
sunglasses **les lunettes**
  de soleil (f)
sunny **ensoleillé**
sunshade **le parasol**
suntan **le bronzage**

suntan lotion
  la lotion solaire
supermarket **le supermarché**
supper **le souper**
supplement **le supplément**
suppository **le suppositoire**
sure **sûr**
suspenders (clothes)
  les bretelles (f)
sweat **la transpiration;**
  (verb) **transpirer**
sweater **le pull, le gilet**
sweatshirt **le sweat-shirt**
sweet (not sour) **sucré**
swim (verb) **nager**
swimming **la natation;** *to go*
  swimming **aller se baigner**
swimming pool **la piscine**
swimming trunks
  le maillot de bain
swimsuit **le maillot de bain**
Swiss **suisse(sse)**
switch **l'interrupteur** (m)
Switzerland **la Suisse**
synagogue **la synagogue**
syringe **la seringue**
syrup **le sirop**

T

table **la table**
tablet **le cachet**
take **prendre**
to go (food) **à emporter**
takeoff **le décollage**
talcum powder **le talc**
talk **la conversation;**
  (verb) **parler**
tall **grand**
tampon **le tampon**
tangerine **la mandarine**
tap (water) **le robinet**
tapestry **la tapisserie**
taxi **le taxi**
tea **le thé**
teacher (secondary)
  le professeur
telephone **le téléphone;**
  (verb) **téléphoner**
telephone box **la cabine**
  téléphonique
television **la télévision**
teller **le guichet**
temperature **la température**
ten **dix**
tennis **le tennis**
tennis shoes **les tennis** (m)
tent **la tente**
tent peg **le piquet de tente**
tent pole **le montant**
  de tente

terminal **le terminal**
terrace **la terrasse**
than **que**
thank (verb) **remercier;** *thank you* **merci;** *thanks* **merci**
that (that one) **ça;** *that bus* **ce bus;** *that man* **cet homme;** *that woman* **cette femme;** *what's that?* **qu'est-ce que c'est?;** *I think that the ...* **je pense que le ...**
the **le/la;** (plural) **les**
theater **le théâtre**
their: *their room* **leur chambre;** *their books* **leurs livres;** *it's theirs* **c'est à eux**
them: *it's them* **ce sont eux/ elles;** *it's for them* **c'est pour eux/elles;** *give it to them* **donnez-le-leur**
then **alors;** (after) **ensuite**
there **là;** *there is/are ...* **il y a ...**
these: *these things* **ces choses;** *these are mine* **ils sont à moi**
they **ils;** (fem) **elles**
thick **épais**
thief **le voleur**
thin **mince, maigre**
think **penser;** *I think so* **je pense que oui;** *I'll think about it* **je vais y penser**
third **troisième**
thirsty: *I'm thirsty* **j'ai soif**
thirteen **treize**
thirty **trente**
this (this one) **ceci;** *this bus* **ce bus;** *this man* **cet homme;** *this woman* **cette femme;** *what's this?* **qu'est-ce que c'est?;** *this is Mr ...* **je vous présente M. ...**
those: *those things* **ces choses-là;** *those are his* **ils sont à lui**
three **trois**
throat **la gorge**
throat lozenges **les pastilles pour la gorge** (f)
through **à travers**
thumbtack **la punaise**
thunderstorm **l'orage** (m)
Thursday **jeudi**
ticket **le billet;** (metro, bus) **le ticket**
ticket collector **le contrôleur**
ticket office **le guichet**
tide **la marée**

tie **la cravate;** (verb) **nouer**
tight **étroit**
tiles, tiling **le carrelage**
time **l'heure** (f); *what's the time?* **quelle heure est-il?**
tip (money) **le pourboire;** (end) **le bout**
tire **le pneu**
tired **fatigué**
tissues **mouchoirs**
to: *to America* **en Amérique;** *to Paris* **à Paris;** *to the station* **à la gare;** *to the center* **au centre;** *to the doctor* **chez le docteur**
toast **le pain grillé**
tobacco **le tabac**
toboggan **le toboggan**
today **aujourd'hui**
together **ensemble**
toilet paper **le papier hygiénique**
tomato **la tomate**
tomorrow **demain;** *see you tomorrow* **à demain**
tongue **la langue**
tonic **le tonic**
tonight **ce soir**
too (also) **aussi;** (excessively) **trop**
tooth **la dent**
toothache **le mal de dents**
toothbrush **la brosse à dents**
toothpaste **le dentifrice**
tour **la visite**
tourist **le/la touriste**
tourist office **le syndicat d'initiative**
towel **la serviette**
tower **la tour**
town **la ville**
town hall **l'hôtel de ville** (m); **la mairie**
toy **le jouet**
tractor **le tracteur**
trade fair **la foire-exposition**
tradition **la tradition**
traffic **la circulation, le trafic**
traffic lights **les feux** (m)
trailer **la remorque**
train **le train**
trainee **le stagiaire**
translate **traduire**
translator **le traducteur**
trash bag **le sac poubelle**
trash can **la poubelle**
travel agency **l'agence de voyages** (f)
tray **le plateau**
tree **l'arbre** (m)

truck **le camion**
true **vrai**
trunk (car) **le coffre**
try **essayer**
Tuesday **mardi**
tunnel **le tunnel**
turn signal **le clignotant**
tweezers **la pince à épiler**
twelve **douze**
twenty **vingt**
two **deux**

U

ugly **laid**
umbrella **le parapluie**
uncle **l'oncle** (m)
under ... **sous ...**
underpants **le slip**
understand **comprendre;** *I understand* **je comprends;** *I don't understand* **je ne comprends pas**
underwear **les sous-vêtements** (f)
university **l'université** (f)
unleaded **sans plomb**
until **jusqu'à**
unusual **inhabituel**
up **en haut;** (upward) **vers le haut;** *up there* **là-haut**
urgent **urgent**
us: *it's us* **c'est nous;** *it's for us* **c'est pour nous;** *give it to us* **donnez-le-nous**
use (verb) **utiliser;** *it's no use* **ça ne sert à rien**
useful **utile**
usual **habituel**
usually **d'habitude**

V

vacancy (room) **la chambre à louer**
vacation **les vacances** (f)
vaccination **la vaccination**
vacuum cleaner **l'aspirateur** (m)
valley **la vallée**
valve **la soupape**
vanilla **la vanille**
vase **le vase**
VCR **le magnétoscope**
veal **le veau**
vegetables **les légumes** (m)
vegetarian (adj) **végétarien**
vehicle **le véhicule**
very **très;** *very much* **beaucoup**

veterinarian **le vétérinaire**
video (film/tape) **la vidéo**
view **la vue**
viewfinder **le viseur**
villa **la villa**
village **le village**
vinegar **le vinaigre**
violin **le violon**
visit **la visite**; (verb: place)
    visiter; (person)
    rendre visite
visitor **le visiteur**
vitamin pill **le comprimé**
    de vitamines
vodka **la vodka**
voice **la voix**
voicemail **la messagerie**
    téléphonique

W

wait **attendre**; wait!
    attendez!
waiter **le serveur**;
    waiter! **garçon!**
waiting room
    la salle d'attente
waitress **la serveuse**;
    waitress! **Mademoiselle!**
Wales **le pays de Galles**
walk (verb) **marcher**; to go for
    a walk **aller se promener**
wall (inside) **la paroi**;
    (outside) **le mur**
wallet **le portefeuille**
want (verb) **vouloir**;
    I would like **je voudrais**
war **la guerre**
wardrobe **l'armoire** (f)
warm **chaud**
was: I was **j'étais**; he was
    il était; she was **elle était**;
    it was **il/elle était**
washer **la rondelle**
washing machine
    la machine à laver
wasp **la guêpe**
watch **la montre**;
    (verb) **regarder**
water **l'eau** (f)
waterfall **la chute d'eau**
water heater **le chauffe-eau**
wave **la vague**; (verb)
    faire signe de la main
wavy (hair) **ondulé**

we **nous**
weather **le temps**
Website **le site web**
wedding **le mariage**
Wednesday **mercredi**
weeds **les mauvais**
    herbes (f)
week **la semaine**
welcome: you're welcome
    je vous en prie
Wellington boots **les boîtes**
    en caoutchouc (f)
were: we were **nous étions**;
    you were **vous étiez**;
    they were **ils/elles étaient**
west **l'ouest**
wet **mouillé**
what? **comment?**; what is it?
    qu'est-ce que c'est?
wheel **la roue**
wheelchair **le fauteuil**
    roulant; **la chaise**
    roulante
when? **quand?**
where? **où?**
whether **si**
which? **lequel?**
whiskey **le whisky**
white **blanc**, (fem) **blanche**
who? **qui?**
why? **pourquoi?**
wide **large**
wife **la femme**
wind **le vent**
window **la fenêtre**
windshield **le pare-brise**
wine **le vin**
wine list **la carte des vins**
wine merchant **le négociant**
    en vins
wing **l'aile** (f)
winter **l'hiver** (m)
with **avec**; with pleasure
    avec plasir
withdraw (verb) **retirer**
without **sans**
witness **le témoin**
woman **la femme**
wood **le bois**
wool **la laine**
word **le mot**
work **le travail**; (verb)
    travailler; (machine, etc.)
    fonctionner
worse **pire**

worst **le pire**
wrapping paper **le papier**
    d'emballage; (for presents)
    le papier cadeau
wrench **la clé anglaise**
wrist **le poignet**
write (verb) **écrire**;
    written by **écrit par**
writing paper
    le papier à lettres
wrong **faux**, (fem) **fausse**

X, Y, Z

X-ray **radio**
X-ray departement
    la salle de radiology
year **l'an** (m); **l'année** (f)
yellow **jaune**
yes **oui**
yesterday **hier**
yet **déjà**; not yet **pas encore**
yogurt **le yaourt**
you (singular informal)
    tu; (plural; singular formal)
    vous
young **jeune**
your (singular informal):
    your book **ton livre**;
    your house **ta maison**;
    your shoes **tes chaussures**;
    it's yours **c'est à toi**;
    (plural; singular formal):
    your house **votre**
    maison; your shoes
    vos chaussures; it's
    yours **c'est à vous**
youth hostel **l'auberge de**
    jeunesse (f)
zipper **la fermeture éclair**
zoo **le zoo**
zucchini **la courgette**

DICTIONARY
French to English

The gender of French nouns listed here is indicated by the abbreviations (m) and (f), for masculine and feminine. Plural nouns are indicated by (m pl) or (f pl). French adjectives (adj) vary according to the gender and number of the word they describe; the masculine form is shown here. In most cases, you add an **-e** to the masculine form to make it feminine. Certain endings use a different rule: masculine adjectives that end in **-x** adopt an **-se** ending in the feminine form, while those that end in **-ien** change to **-ienne**. Some feminine adjectives that do not follow these rules are shown here and follow the abbreviation (fem). For the plural form, a (silent) **-s** is usually added.

A

à: *at:* **à la poste** *at the post office;* **à trois heures** *at 3 o'clock;* **à côté de** *beside;* **à demain** *see you tomorrow;* **à emporter** *to go* (food); **à travers** *through*
abat-jour (m) *lampshade*
abricot (m) *apricot*
accélérateur (m) *accelerator*
accident (m) *accident*
acheter *to buy*
adaptateur (m) *adapter* (voltage)
addition (f) *check* (in restaurant)
adhésif (m) *adhesive*
adresse (f) *address*
adresse électronique (f) *email address*
aéroglisseur (m) *hovercraft*
aéroport (m) *airport*
affaire (f) *bargain*
affaires (f pl) *business*
affiche (f) *poster* (outside)
affreux *awful*
agence de voyages (f) *travel agency*
agenda (m) *planner*
agent (m) *agent*
agneau (m) *lamb*
agrafeuse (f) *stapler*
agrandissement (m) *enlargement*
aide (f) *help*
aider *to help*
aiguille (f) *needle;* **aiguille à tricoter** *knitting needle*
ail (m) *garlic*
aile (f) *wing*
ailleurs *somewhere else*
aimer *to like/love;* **j'aime nager** *I like swimming;* **je n'aime pas** *I don't like*

air (m) *air*
alcool (m) *alcohol*
Algérie (f) *Algeria*
algérien(ne) *Algerian*
allée (f) *path*
Allemagne (f) *Germany*
allemand(e) *German*
aller *to go*
aller chercher *to get* (fetch)
allergique *allergic*
aller patiner *to go ice-skating*
aller retour (m) *round-trip ticket*
aller simple (m) *one-way ticket*
allez-vous en! *go away!*
allumage (m) *ignition*
allumette (f) *match* (light)
alors *well then*
Alpes: les Alpes (m pl) *Alps*
amant (m) *lover*
ambassade (f) *embassy*
ambulance (f) *ambulance*
amer *bitter*
américain(e) *American*
Amérique (f) *America*
ami(e) *friend*
amical *friendly*
amour (m) *love*
amphithéâtre (m) *lecture hall*
ampoule (f) *blister; light bulb*
an (m) *year*
ananas (m) *pineapple*
Andorre *Andorra*
anglais(e) *English*
Angleterre (f) *England*
animaux (familiers) (m pl) *pets*
animé *busy* (street)
année (f) *year*
anniversaire (m) *birthday*
annuaire (m) *directory* (telephone)

antigel (m) *antifreeze*
antiseptique (m) *antiseptic*
août *August*
apéritif (m) *aperitif*
appareil acoustique (m) *hearing aid*
appareil-photo (m) *camera*
appartement (m) *apartment*
appât (m) *bait*
appétit (m) *appetite*
apprendre *to learn*
après *after*
après-midi (m) *afternoon*
après-rasage (m) *aftershave*
araignée (f) *spider*
arbre (m) *tree*
arbre à cames (m) *camshaft*
architecture (f) *architecture*
arête (f) *fish bone*
argent (m) *cash; money; silver* (metal)
argenté *silver* (color)
armoire (f) *wardrobe*
arrêt de bus (m) *bus stop*
arrière (m) *back* (not front)
arrivée (f) *arrival*
arriver *to arrive*
art (m) *art*
artiste (m) *artist*
ascenseur (m) *elevator*
aspirateur (m) *vacuum cleaner*
aspirine (f) *aspirin*
assez *enough; fairly*
assiette (f) *plate*
assurance (f) *insurance*
asthmatique *asthmatic*
attaché-case (m) *briefcase*
attendez! *wait!*
attendre *to wait*

attention! *careful!*
atterrir *to land*
attirant *attractive*
au: au café *at the café;*
　au revoir *goodbye*
auberge (f) *inn*
auberge de jeunesse (f)
　youth hostel
aucun *not any; none*
au-dessus de *over (above)*
aujourd'hui *today*
aussi *too (also)*
Australie (f) *Australia*
australien(ne) *Australian*
automatique *automatic*
automne (m) *autumn*
autoroute (f) *highway,*
　freeway
autre: autre chose
　something else
avance (f) *advance*
avant *before*
avec *with;* **avec plaisir**
　I'd love to
averse (f) *shower (rain)*
aveugle *blind (cannot see)*
avion (m) *aircraft*
avocat (m) *avocado*
avocat(e) *lawyer*
avoir *to have*
avril *April*

B

bac (m) *ferry (small)*
bagages (m pl) *luggage;*
　baggage; **bagages à main**
　(m pl) *carry-on luggage*
baigner: aller se baigner
　to go swimming
bain (m) *bath*
balai (m) *broom*
balcon (m) *balcony*
balle (f) *ball (tennis, etc.)*
ballon (m) *ball (soccer, etc.)*
banane (f) *banana*
bandage (m) *bandage*
banlieue (f) *suburbs*
banque (f) *bank*
bar (m) *bar (place)*
barbe (f) *beard*
barbecue (m) *barbecue*
barque (f) *rowboat*
bas (m) *stockings; low (adj);*
　en bas *down*
bateau (m) *boat; ship;*
　bateau à moteur (m)
　motorboat; **bateau à**
　vapeur (m) *steamer*
bâtiment (m) *building*
bâton de ski (m) *ski pole*

batterie (f) *battery (car)*
baume après-shampooing
　(m) *conditioner (hair)*
beau, (fem) **belle** *beautiful*
bébé (m) *baby*
bêche (f) *spade (garden)*
beige *beige*
beignet (m) *doughnut*
belge *Belgian*
Belgique: la Belgique
　Belgium
bénéfices (m pl) *profits*
béquilles (f pl) *crutches*
besoin: avoir besoin de
　to need; **j'ai besoin de ...**
　I need ...
beurre (m) *butter*
bibliothèque (f) *library*
bicyclette (f) *bicycle*
bien sûr *of course*
bien! *good!;* **ça vous va bien**
　it suits you
bière (f) *beer*
bijouterie (f) *jeweler*
billet (m) *ticket; bank note*
biscuit (m) *cookie*
blanc, (fem) **blanche** *white*
blanchisserie (f)
　laundry (place)
blême *pale*
blessure (f) *injury*
bleu (m) *bruise; blue (adj)*
bloc notes (m) *notepad*
blond (adj) *blond*
bœuf (m) *beef*
boire *to drink;* **vous voulez**
　boire quelque chose?
　would you like something
　to drink?
bois (m) *wood*
boisson (f) *drink*
boîte (f) *box;* **boîte à**
　lettres *mailbox;* **boîte**
　de chocolats *box*
　of chocolates; **boîte**
　de conserve *can*
　(vessel); **boîte de nuit**
　nightclub; **boîte de**
　vitesses *gearbox*
boîtes en caoutchouc (f pl)
　Wellington boots
bol (m) *bowl*
bon, (fem) **bonne** *good*
bonbon (m) *sweet*
　(confectionery); **bonbons**
　à la menthe (m pl)
　peppermints
bondé *crowded*
bonjour *hello*
bon marché *inexpensive;*
　cheap

bonne chance! *good luck!*
bonsoir *good evening*
bord (m) *side (edge)*
botte (f) *boot (footwear)*
bouche (f) *mouth*
boucherie (f) *butcher shop*
bouchon (m) *plug (sink);*
　cork
boucles (f pl) *curls*
boucles d'oreille
　(f pl) *earrings*
bouger *to move;* **ne bougez**
　pas! *don't move!*
bougie (f) *spark plug; candle*
bouilli *boiled*
bouillir *to boil*
bouilloire (f) *kettle*
boulangerie (f) *bread shop*
bout (m) *tip, end*
bouteille (f) *bottle*
bouton (m) *button;*
　boutons de manchette
　(m pl) *cufflinks*
bracelet (m) *bracelet*
branche (f) *branch*
bras (m) *arm*
Bretagne: la Bretagne
　Brittany
bretelles (f pl)
　suspenders (clothes)
briquet (m) *lighter*
britannique *British*
broche (f) *brooch*
brochure (f) *brochure*
broderie (f) *embroidery*
bronzage (m) *suntan*
bronzer: se faire bronzer
　to sunbathe
brosse (f) *brush;* **brosse à**
　dents (f) *toothbrush*
brosser *to brush*
brouillard (m) *fog*
brûler *to burn*
brûlure (f) *burn*
Bruxelles *Brussels*
bruyant *noisy*
budget (m) *budget*
bunker (m) *bunker*
bureau (m) *desk; office*
bureau de location (m)
　box office
bus (m) *bus*

C

ça *that (that one)*
cabine téléphonique (f)
　telephone booth
cacahuètes (f pl) *peanuts*
cachet (m) *tablet*
cadeau (m) *gift*

cadenas (m) *padlock*
cadre (m) *executive (in company)*
cafard (m) *cockroach*
café (m) *café; coffee;* **café crème** *coffee with milk;* **café soluble** *instant coffee*
cage (f) *cage*
caisse (f) *checkout (supermarket)*
calculette (f) *calculator*
cambriolage (m) *burglary*
caméscope (m) *camcorder*
camion (m) *truck*
campagne (f) *countryside*
camping-car (m) *camper van*
Canada (m) *Canada*
canadien(ne) *Canadian*
canal (m) *canal*
canif (m) *penknife*
canne à pêche (f) *fishing rod*
canoë (m) *canoe*
caoutchouc (m) *rubber (material)*
capot (m) *car hood*
capsule (f) *cap (bottle)*
caravane (f) *camper trailer*
carburateur (m) *carburetor*
carnet (m) *notebook;* **carnet de chèques** (m) *checkbook*
carotte (f) *carrot*
carpette (f) *rug (mat)*
carré *square (adj: shape)*
carreau *diamonds (cards)*
carrelage (m) *tiles, tiling*
carte (f) *menu; card; map;* **carte bancaire** *debit card;* **carte de crédit** *credit card;* **carte d'embarquement** *boarding pass;* **carte des vins** *wine list;* **carte de visite** *business card;* **carte postale** *postcard;* **carte téléphonique** *phone card*
casquette (f) *cap (hat)*
cassé *broken*
casserole (f) *saucepan*
cassette (f) *cassette*
cassis (m) *black currant*
cathédrale (f) *cathedral*
cave (f) *cellar*
ce (bus) *that (bus)*
ceci *this (this one)*
ceinture (f) *belt;* **ceinture de sécurité** *seat belt*
célibataire *single (unmarried)*
cellule photoélectrique (f) *light meter*
cendrier (m) *ashtray*
cent *hundred*

centre (m) *center;* **centre sportif** (m) *sports center*
centre-ville (m) *down-town, town center*
cerise (f) *cherry*
certificat (m) *certificate*
ces (choses) *these (things)*
c'est *it's;* **c'est tout** *that's all*
cet (homme) *that (man)*
cette (femme) *that (woman)*
chaise (f) *chair*
châle (m) *shawl*
chambre (f) *bedroom;* **chambre à louer** *vacancy;* **chambre pour deux personnes** *double room;* **chambre simple** *single room*
chambre à air (f) *inner tube*
champ (m) *field (farming)*
champignon (m) *mushroom*
chance (f) *luck*
changer *to change (money);* **se changer** *to change (clothes)*
chanson (f) *song*
chanter *to sing*
chapeau (m) *hat*
chaque *each; every*
charcuterie (f) *delicatessen*
chargeur (m) *charger*
chariot (m) *cart*
charpentier (m) *carpenter*
chat (m) *cat*
château (m) *castle*
chaud *hot; warm;* **j'ai chaud** *I feel hot*
chauffage (m) *heating;* **chauffage central** *central heating*
chauffe-eau (m) *boiler; water heater*
chaussettes (f pl) *socks*
chaussures (f pl) *shoes;* **chaussures de ski** (f pl) *ski boots*
chauve *bald*
chef (m) *manager;* **chef d'orchestre** *conductor (orchestra);* **chef de train** *conductor (train)*
chemin (m) *path*
chemin de fer (m) *railroad*
cheminée (f) *fireplace; chimney*
chemise (f) *shirt;* **chemise de nuit** *nightgown*
chemisier (m) *blouse*
chèque (m) *check;*
cher *expensive;* **pas cher** *inexpensive*

cheveux (m pl) *hair;* **les cheveux longs/courts** *long/short hair*
cheville (f) *ankle*
chez *at home;* **chez moi;** *at my house;* **chez vous** *at your place*
chien (m) *dog*
chiffon à poussière (m) *duster*
chiffres (m pl) *figures*
chips (f pl) *chips*
chocolat (m) *chocolate*
chou (m) *cabbage*
chou-fleur (m) *cauliflower*
chute d'eau (f) *waterfall*
ciel (m) *sky*
cigare (m) *cigar*
cigarette (f) *cigarette*
cimetière (m) *cemetery*
cinéma (m) *movie theater, cinema*
cinq *five*
cinquante *fifty*
cintre (m) *coathanger*
cirage (m) *shoe polish*
circulation (f) *traffic*
ciseaux (m pl) *scissors*
citron (m) *lemon;* **citron vert** *lime*
clair *clear; light (not dark)*
classe (f) *class*
clavier (m) *keyboard*
clé (f) *key;* **clé anglaise** (f) *wrench*
clignotant (m) *turn signal*
climatisation (f) *air conditioning*
cloche (f) *bell (church)*
clou (m) *nail (metal)*
cocktail (m) *cocktail party*
code (m) *PIN*
code de la route (m) *highway code*
code postal (m) *postal (ZIP) code*
cœur (m) *heart;* **problème au cœur** *heart condition;* **cœurs** (m pl) *hearts (cards)*
coffre (m) *trunk (car)*
cognac (m) *brandy*
coiffeur (m) *hairdresser; barber's*
coin (m) *corner*
col (m) *collar*
colis (m) *parcel*
collants (m pl) *pantyhose*
colle (f) *glue*
collection (f) *collection (stamps, etc.)*

collier (m) *collar; necklace*
colline (f) *hill*
combien? *how much?;*
   combien ça coûte?
   how much does it cost?
comme *like* (similar to)
commencer *to start*
comment? *how?;* comment
   allez-vous? *how are you?;*
   comment est-ce que ça
   s'appelle? *what's it called?;*
   comment vous appelez-
   vous? *what's your name?*
commerçant(e) *shopkeeper*
commissariat (m)
   police station
commode (f) *dresser*
compagnie (f)
   company; compagnie
   aérienne *airline*
compartiment (m)
   compartment
complet *full*
compliqué *complicated*
comprendre *to understand;*
   je comprends *I*
   understand; je ne
   comprends pas *I don't*
   understand
comprimé (m) *pill;*
   comprimé de vitamines
   vitamin pill
comptable (m/f) *accountant*
compte: à mon compte
   self-employed
concert (m) *concert*
concierge (m/f) *caretaker*
concombre (m) *cucumber*
conducteur (m) *driver*
conduire *to drive*
conférence (f) *conference*
confiseur (m) *candy store*
confiture (f) *jam*
congélateur (m) *freezer*
connaître *to know* (person)
consigne automatique (f)
   luggage lockers
constructeur (m) *builder*
consulat (m) *consulate*
consultant(e) *consultant*
contraceptif (m)
   contraceptive
contre *against*
contrôle des passeports
   (m) *passport control*
contrôleur (m) *ticket collector*
conversation (f) *talk*
copieur (m) *photocopier*
coquille (f) *shell*
corde (f) *rope; string*
   (guitar, etc.)

cordonnerie (f) *shoemaker*
corne (f) *horn* (animal)
corps (m) *body*
correspondant (m)
   pen pal
corse *Corsican*
Corse: la Corse *Corsica*
costume (m) *suit*
côtelette (f) *chop* (food)
coton (m) *cotton;* coton
   hydrophile *cotton balls*
cou (m) *neck*
couche (f) *diaper;*
   couches à jeter (f pl)
   disposable diapers
coude (m) *elbow*
coudre *to sew*
couette (f) *comforter*
   (bedding)
couleur (f) *color*
couloir (m) *corridor*
coup de soleil (m)
   sunburn
coupe (de cheveux) (f)
   haircut
couper *to cut, chop*
coupure (f) *cut*
courant (m) *current*
courgette (f) *zucchini*
courir *to run*
courroie du ventilateur
   (f) *fan belt*
courses (f pl) *shopping;*
   to go shopping faire
   les courses
court *short*
couscoussier (m) *steamer*
   (cooking)
cousin (m) *cousin*
couteau (m) *knife*
coûter *to cost*
couverture (f) *blanket; rug*
crabe (m) *crab*
crampe (f) *cramp*
cravate (f) *tie*
crayon (m) *pencil*
crème (f) *cream;*
   crème anti-insecte (f)
   insect repellent cream
crêpe (f) *crêpe*
crevaison (f) *puncture*
   (tire)
crevette (f) *shrimp*
crier *to cry* (shout)
croisière (f) *cruise*
crustacés (m) *shellfish*
cuillère (f) *spoon*
cuir (m) *leather*
cuire *to bake*
cuisine (f) *kitchen*
cuisinier (m) *cook*

cuisinière (f) *stove*
curry (m) *curry*

D

d'accord *OK*
danger *danger;* sans danger
   safe
dans *in*
danse (f) *dance*
danser *to dance*
de *of*
début (m) *start* (beginning)
débutant(e) *beginner*
décapsuleur (m)
   bottle opener
décembre *December*
décollage (m) *takeoff*
décolorer *to bleach*
décorateur (m) *decorator*
dehors *outside*
déjà *yet; already*
déjeuner (m) *lunch*
delco (m) *distributor* (car)
demain *tomorrow*
démaquillant (m)
   skin cleanser
déménager *to move*
   (change homes)
demi *half;* une demi-heure
   half an hour
demi-pension (f) *half- board*
dent (f) *tooth*
dentelle (f) *lace*
dentier (m) *dentures*
dentifrice (m) *toothpaste*
dentiste (m/f) *dentist*
déodorant (m) *deodorant*
départ (m) *departures*
département (f) *department*
dépliant (m) *leaflet*
déposition (f) *statement*
déraper *skid* (verb)
dernier *last* (final);
   la semaine dernière
   last week
derrière *behind*
descendre *to get off*
   (bus, etc.)
designer (m) *designer*
désolé: je suis désolé (e)
   I'm sorry
desserts (m pl) *desserts*
détritus (m) *garbage*
deux *two;* les deux *both*
deuxième *second* (in series)
devant *in front of*
développer *to develop*
d'habitude *usually*
diabétique *diabetic*
diamant (m) *diamond* (jewel)

diarrhée (f) *diarrhea*
dictionnaire (m) *dictionary*
diesel (m) *diesel*
différent *different;* **c'est différent** *that's different*
difficile *difficult*
dimanche *Sunday*
dîner (m) *dinner*
dire *to say;* **qu'avez-vous dit?** *what did you say?;* **comment dit-on ...?** *how do you say ...?;* **qu'est-ce que cela veut dire?** *what does this mean?*
directeur (m) *director*
discothèque (m) *disco*
disquaire (m) *record store*
disque (m) *record (music);* **disque compact** (m) *CD (compact disc)*
distributeur automatique (m) *ATM*
divertissement (m) *entertainment*
divorcé *divorced*
dix *ten*
dix-huit *eighteen*
dix-neuf *nineteen*
dix-sept *seventeen*
docteur (m) *doctor*
document (m) *document*
doigt (m) *finger*
dois: je dois ... *I must ...*
dollar (m) *dollar*
donner *give*
dormir *to sleep*
dos (m) *back (body)*
douane (f) *customs*
doubler *to overtake (in a car)*
douche (f) *shower (bath)*
douleur (f) *ache; pain*
douze *twelve*
drap (m) *sheet*
drapeau (m) *flag*
draps (m pl) *bed linen*
droit (m) *law*
droite *right (not left)*
drôle *funny*
dunes (f pl) *sand dunes*
dur *hard*

E

eau (f) *water;* **eau gazeuse** *sparkling water;* **eau minérale** *mineral water;* **eau potable** *drinking water;* **eau de Javel** *bleach*
échanger *to exchange*
écharpe (f) *scarf*
échecs (m pl) *chess*

école (f) *school*
Ecosse: l'Ecosse (f) *Scotland*
écouteurs (m) *headphones*
écran (m) *screen*
écrevisse (f) *crayfish (freshwater)*
écrire *to write;* **écrit par ...** *written by ...*
écrou (m) *nut (for bolt)*
église (f) *church*
élastique (m) *elastic band;* *elastic* (adj)
électricien(ne) *electrician*
électricité (f) *electricity*
électrique *electric*
elle *she*
elles *they (fem)*
email (m) *email*
embrayage (m) *clutch*
émeraude (f) *emerald*
emplacement (m) *pitch*
emploi du temps (m) *schedule*
en *in;* **en France** *in France*
enchanté(e) *pleased to meet you*
encore: encore un café *another cup of coffee*
encre (f) *ink*
endormi *asleep*
endroit (m) *place*
enfant (m) *child*
enfin! *at last!*
ennuyeux *boring*
enregistrement (m) *check-in;* **enregistrement des bagages** *baggage check-in*
ensemble *together*
ensoleillé *sunny*
ensuite *then (after)*
entendre *hear*
entre ... *between ...*
entrée (f) *entrance*
entrées (f pl) *starters*
enveloppe (f) *envelope*
envie: j'ai envie de ... *I feel like ...*
environ *about*
envoyer *to send*
épais *thick*
épaule (f) *shoulder*
épicerie (f) *grocery store*
épileptique *epileptic*
épinards (m) *spinach*
épingle (f) *pin;* **épingle de nourrice** *safety pin*
erreur (f) *mistake*
escalier (m) *stairs; staircase;* **escalier roulant** *escalator*
Espagne: l'Espagne (f) *Spain*

espagnol *Spanish*
essayer *to try*
essence (f) *gasoline*
essieu (m) *axle*
est (m) *east*
est *is;* **il/elle est** *he/she is;* **c'est** *it is*
estimation (f) *estimate*
estomac (m) *stomach*
et *and*
étage (m) *floor (story)*
été (m) *summer*
étiquette (f) *label*
étoile (f) *star*
étouffant *stuffy*
étranger (m) *foreigner*
étroit *narrow; tight*
étudiant (m) *student*
eux: c'est à eux *it's theirs;* **c'est pour eux/elles** *it's for them*
evanouir *to faint*
évier (m) *sink*
excédent de bagages (m) *excess baggage*
excellent *excellent*
excursion (f) *excursion*
exemple (m) *example*
exposition (f) *exhibition*
exprès *deliberately*
extérieure (m) *exterior;* *exterior* (adj)
exterior **extincteur** (m) *fire extinguisher*

F

face: en face de *opposite*
facile *easy*
façon: d'une façon ou d'une autre *somehow*
facteur (m) *mail carrier*
facture (f) *invoice*
faim: j'ai faim *I'm hungry*
faire *to do; make;* **faire de autostop** *to hitchhike;* **faire du jogging** *to jog;* **faire enregistrer ses bagages** *to check in;* **faire la cuisine** *to cook;* **faire la queue** *to stand in line (verb);* **faire signe de la main** *to wave*
fan (m/f) *fan (enthusiast)*
fantastique *fantastic*
farine (f) *flour*
fatigué *tired*
fauteuil (m) *armchair;* **fauteuil roulant** (m) *wheelchair*

faux, (fem) **fausse** *wrong*
félicitations! *congratulations!*
femme (f) *woman; wife;*
   femme de chambre
   maid; **femme de**
   ménages *cleaner*
fenêtre (f) *window*
fer à repasser (m) *iron*
   (for clothes)
ferme (f) *farm*
fermé *closed*
fermer *to close*
fermeture éclair (f) *zipper*
fermier (m) *farmer*
ferry (m) *ferry (large)*
fête (f) *party (celebration)*
feu (m) *fire;* **feu d'artifice**
   fireworks; **feu de camp**
   campfire
feuille (f) *leaf*
feutre (m) *felt-tip pen*
feux (m pl) *lights; traffic lights;*
   feux de position (m pl)
   sidelights
fevrier *February*
fiancé *engaged (couple)*
fiancé(e) *fiancé(e)*
ficelle (f) *string (cord)*
fièvre (f) *fever*
figue (f) *fig*
fille (f) *girl; daughter*
film (m) *film*
fils (m) *son*
fin (f) *end*
fini *over (finished)*
flash (m) *flash (camera)*
fleur (f) *flower*
fleuriste (f) *florist*
fleuve (m) *river (big)*
flûte (f) *flute*
foie (m) *liver*
foire (f) *fair;*
   foire-exposition *trade fair*
foncé *dark;* **bleu foncé**
   dark blue
fonctionner *function*
   (machine, etc.)
fond (m) *bottom*
football (m) *soccer*
forêt (f) *forest*
formulaire de demande
   (m) *application form*
fort *loud; strong*
   (person, drink)
fou, (fem) **folle** *mad*
foulard (m) *headscarf*
four (m) *oven*
fourchette (f) *fork*
frais, (fem) **fraîche** *cool*
fraise (f) *strawberry*
framboise (f) *raspberry*

français(e) *French*
France: la France *France*
frange (f) *fringe*
frein (m) *brake;*
   frein à main *handbrake*
freiner *to brake*
frère (m) *brother*
frigo (m) *refrigerator*
frire *to fry*
frit *fried*
frites (f pl) *chips*
froid (adj) *cold*
fromage (m) *cheese*
fromagerie (f) *cheese shop*
frontière (f) *border*
fruit (m) *fruit*
fruits de mer (m pl) *seafood*
fumée (f) *smoke*
fumer *to smoke*
fusil (m) *rifle*

G
....

galerie d'art (f)
   art gallery
gamelle (f) *animal's*
   bowl
gants (m pl) *gloves*
garage (m) *garage*
garagiste (m) *mechanic*
garantie (f) *guarantee*
garantir *to guarantee*
garçon (m) *boy;*
   garçon! *waiter!*
gare (f) *station;*
   gare routière (f)
   bus station
garer *to park*
garniture (f) *filling (in*
   sandwich, cake)
gâteau (m) *cake*
gauche *left (not right)*
gaz (m) *gas;* **gaz à briquet**
   (m) *lighter fluid*
gazoile (m) *diesel*
gel (m) *gel; frost;*
   gel douche (m)
   shower gel
gênant *embarrassing*
genou (m) *knee*
gens (m pl) *people*
gentil *friendly; kind*
gilet (m) *sweater*
gin (m) *gin*
gingembre (m) *ginger*
glace (f) *ice; ice cream*
golf (m) *golf*
gomme (f) *eraser*
gorge (f) *throat*
goût (m) *flavor*
goutes (f pl) *drops*

gouttière (f) *gutter*
gouvernement (m)
   government
grand *big; large; tall;*
   grand magasin (m)
   department store
Grande-Bretagne (f)
   Great Britain
grand-mère (f) *grandmother*
grand-père (m) *grandfather*
grands-parents (m pl)
   grandparents
gras (m) *fat (on meat, etc.)*
gratuit *free (of charge)*
grenier (m) *attic*
gril (m) *grill*
grillé (e) *grilled*
gris *gray*
gros, (fem) **grosse** (adj) *fat*
grotte (f) *cave*
groupe (m) *group; band*
   (musicians)
guêpe (f) *wasp*
guerre (f) *war*
gueule de bois (f) *hangover*
guichet (m) *cashier, teller;*
   ticket office
guide (m) *guide; guide book;*
   guide de conversation
   (m) *phrase book*
guitare (f) *guitar*

H
....

habituel *ordinary; usual*
hache (f) *ax*
haie (f) *hedge*
hamburger (m) *hamburger*
hamster (m) *hamster*
handicapé *disabled*
haricots (m pl) *beans*
haut *high;* **en haut** *up;*
   vers la haut *upward;*
   là-haut *up there*
hébergement (m)
   accommodation
hépatite (f) *hepatitis*
herbe (f) *grass*
heure (f) *hour; time*
heures d'ouverture (f pl)
   opening times
heureux *glad; happy*
hier *yesterday*
histoire (f) *history*
hiver (m) *winter*
homard (m) *lobster*
homéopathie *homeopathy*
homme (m) *man*
homosexuel *gay*
honnête *honest*
hôpital (m) *hospital*

horaire (f) *schedule* (train, bus)
horloge (f) *clock*
horrible *horrible*
hors-taxe *duty-free*
hôte (m) *host*
hôtel (m) *hotel*
hôtel de ville (m) *town hall*
hôtesse(f) *hostess;* **hôtesse de air** *flight attendant*
hoverport (m) *hoverport*
huile (f) *oil*
huit *eight*
huître (f) *oyster*
hydrofoil (m) *hydrofoill*

I

identification (f) *identification*
il *he; it* (m)
île (f) *island;* **les îles Anglo-Normandes** *Channel Islands*
ils *they* (m); **ils sont** *they are*
il y a ... *there is/are ...*
immédiatement *immediately*
imperméable (m) *raincoat*
impossible *impossible*
imprimante (f) *printer*
incendie (m) *fire* (blaze)
indigestion (f) *indigestion*
infection (f) *infection*
infirmier, (fem) **infirmière** *nurse*
information (f) *information*
informations (f pl) *news* (TV)
ingénierie (f) *engineering*
ingénieur (m) *engineer*
inhabituel *unusual*
insecte (m) *insect*
insomnie (f) *insomnia*
instrument de musique (m) *musical instrument*
intelligent *clever*
intéressant *interesting*
internet (m) *Internet*
interprète (m) *interpreter*
interpréter *to interpret*
interrupteur (m) *switch*
intoxication alimentaire (f) *food poisoning*
invitation (f) *invitation*
invité(e) *guest*
irlandais(e) *Irish*

Irlande (f) *Ireland*
Italie (f) *Italy*
italien(ne) *Italian*
ivre *drunk*

J

jamais *never*
jambe (f) *leg;* **jambe cassée** (f) *broken leg*
jambon (m) *ham*
janvier *January*
jardin (m) *garden, yard;* **jardin public** (m) *park*
jardinerie (f) *garden center*
jaune *yellow*
jazz (m) *jazz*
je l; je suis *I am;* **je voudrais** *I would like*
jeans (m pl) *jeans*
jeu (m) *game:* **jeux vidéos** (m pl) *computer games*
jeu de cartes (m) *pack of cards*
jeudi *Thursday*
jeune *young*
joli *nice; pretty* (place, etc.)
jouer *to play*
jouet (m) *toy*
jour (m) *day*
journal (m) *newspaper*
joyeux anniversaire! *happy birthday!*
juillet *July*
juin *June*
jupe (f) *skirt*
jupon (m) *slip*
jus (m) *juice:* **jus d'orange** *orange juice;* **jus de fruit** (m) *fruit juice*
jusqu'à *until*
juste *right; fair* (correct); **ce n'est pas juste** *it's not fair*
juste un peu *just a little*

K, L

kilo (m) *kilo*
kilomètre (m) *kilometer* (0.62 miles)
klaxon (m) *horn* (car)
la *the* (fem)
là *there;* **il n'est pas là** *he's out*
là-bas *over there*
lac (m) *lake*
lacet (m) *shoelace*
laid *ugly*

laine(f) *wool*
laisse (f) *lead*
lait (m) *milk*
lames de rasoir (f pl) *razor blades*
lampe (f) *lamp;* **lampe de bureau** *reading lamp;* **lampe de chevet** *bedside lamp;* **lampe de poche** (f) *flashlight*
landau (m) *baby carriage*
langouste (f) *crayfish* (saltwater)
langue (f) *language; tongue*
lapin (m) *rabbit*
laque (f) *hairspray*
large *wide*
lavabo (m) *basin* (sink)
laverie automatique (f) *laundromat*
lave-vaisselle (m) *dishwasher*
laxatif (m) *laxative*
le *the* (m)
leçon (f) *lesson*
lecteur de cassettes (m) *cassette player*
léger *light* (not heavy)
légumes (m pl) *vegetables*
lent *slow*
lentilles *lenses* (f pl); **lentilles rigides** *hard lenses;* **lentilles semi-souples** *gas-permeable lenses;* **lentilles souples** *soft lenses*
lequel, (fem) **laquelle:** **lequel?** *which?;* **n'importe lequel** *either of them*
les *the* (plural)
lessive(f) *laundry detergent*
lettre (f) *letter*
leur: leur chambre *their room;* **leurs livres** *their books*
levée (f) *mail pickup*
lever: se lever *to get up*
levier de vitesse (m) *gearshift*
librairie (f) *bookshop*
libre *free* (at liberty)
lime à ongles (f) *nail file*
limitation de vitesse (f) *speed limit*
limonade (f) *lemon soda*
linge (m) *laundry* (clothes)
lingettes (f pl) *baby wipes*
liqueur (f) *liqueur*
liquide: payer en liquide *to pay cash*

lire *to read*
liste (f) *list*
lit (m) *bed*; **lit d'enfant** (m) *crib*
litérature (f) *literature*
litre (m) *liter (quart)*
livraison (f) *delivery*
livre (m) *book; pound (weight)*
loin *far*
long, (fem) **longue** *long*
longueur (f) *length*
lotion solaire (f) *suntan lotion*
louer *to rent*
lourd *heavy*
luge (f) *sled*
lumière (f) *light*
lundi *Monday*
lune (f) *moon;* **lune de miel** *honeymoon*
lunettes (f pl) *glasses;* **lunettes de soleil** *sunglasses*
Luxembourg (m) *Luxembourg*

M

ma: ma maison *my house*
machine à laver (f) *washing machine*
maçon (m) *bricklayer*
Madame *Mrs.*
Mademoiselle! *waitress!*
magasin (m) *shop;* **magasin d'antiquités** *antique shop*
magnètoscope (m) *VCR*
mai *May*
maigre *thin*
maillot de bain (m) *swimsuit; swimming trunks*
main (f) *hand*
maintenant *now*
mairie (f) *town hall*
mais *but*
maison (f) *house*
maître de conférences (m) *associate professor*
malade *ill*
mal à estomac (m) *stomachache*
mal à la tête (m) *headache*
mal de dents (m) *toothache*
mal de ventre (m) *stomachache*
manche (f) *sleeve*
Manche: la Manche *Channel*
mandarine (f) *tangerine*

manger *to eat*
manteau (m) *coat*
maquillage (m) *makeup*
marché (m) *market*
marcher *to walk*
mardi *Tuesday*
marée (f) *tide*
margarine (f) *margarine*
mari (m) *husband*
mariage (m) *wedding*
marié *married*
marmelade d'oranges (f) *marmalade*
marron *brown*
mars *March*
marteau (m) *hammer*
mascara (m) *mascara*
mât (m) *mast*
match (m) *match, game (sport)*
matelas (m) *mattress;* **matelas pneumatique** *air mattress*
matin (m) *morning*
mauvais *bad; poor (bad quality);* **mauvais herbes** (f) *weeds*
mécanicien (m) *mechanic*
médecin (m) *doctor*
médicaments (m pl) *medication*
médicine (m) *medicine (subject)*
Méditerranée: la Méditerranée (f) *Mediterranean*
méduse (f) *jellyfish*
meilleur: le meilleur *the best*
melon (m) *melon*
même *same;* **le/la même ...** *the same ...;* **la même chose, s'il vous plaît** *the same again, please*
menu (m) *set menu*
mer (f) *sea*
merci *thank you*
mercredi *Wednesday*
mère (f) *mother*
mes: mes chaussures *my shoes*
message (m) *message*
messagerie (f): **messagerie électronique** *email;* **messagerie téléphonique** *voicemail*
messe (f) *mass (church)*
métro (m) *underground*
mettre *to put*

meublé *furnished*
meubles (m pl) *furniture*
micro-ondes (m) *microwave*
midday *noon*
miel (m) *honey*
mieux *better*
milieu (m) *middle*
mince *thin*
minuit *midnight*
minute (f) *minute*
miroir (m) *mirror*
mobylette (f) *moped*
mode (f) *fashion*
modem (m) *modem*
moi *me;* **c'est moi** *it's me;* **c'est pour moi;** *it's for me;* **c'est à moi** *it's mine*
moins *less*
mois (m) *month*
mon: mon livre *my book*
moniteur (m) *monitor (computer)*
monnaie (f) *change (money)*
monsieur *sir;* **Monsieur** *Mr.*
montagne (f) *mountain*
montant de tente (m) *tent pole*
monter *to get on (bus, etc.)*
montre (f) *watch*
monument (m) *monument*
morceau (m) *piece*
mordre *to bite (dog)*
morsure (f) *bite (by dog)*
mort *dead*
mot (m) *word;* **mot de passe** (m) *password*
moteur (m) *engine (car)*
moto (f) *motorcycle*
mou *soft*
mouche (f) *fly (insect)*
mouchoir (m) *handkerchief*
mouchoirs *tissues*
mouillé *wet*
moules (f pl) *mussels*
mourir *to die*
mousse (f) *mousse (hair);* **mousse à raser** (f) *shaving foam*
moustache (f) *mustache*
moustique (m) *mosquito*
moutarde (f) *mustard*
mur (m) *wall (outside)*
mûr *ripe*
mûre (f) *blackberry*
musée (m) *museum;* **musée d'art** *art gallery*
musicien (m) *musician;*

musicien des rues
street musician
musique (f) *music;*
musique classique
classical music; **musique**
folklorique *folk*
music; **musique pop**
pop music

N

nager *to swim*
natation (f) *swimming*
navette (pour aéroport) (f)
airport bus
né (e): je suis né (e)
en ... *I was born in ...*
nécessaire *necessary;*
ce n'est pas nécessaire
that's not necessary
négatif (m) *negative* (photo)
négociant en vins (m)
wine merchant
neige (f) *snow*
neuf *nine*
neuf, (fem) neuve *new*
neveu (m) *nephew*
nez (m) *nose*
ni: ni un ni autre
neither of them;
ni ... ni ... *neither ...*
nor ...
nièce (f) *niece*
nier *to deny*
noir *black*
noix (f) *nut* (fruit)
nom (m) *name;*
nom de famille (m)
last name
nombre (m) *number*
(amount)
non *no*
nord (m) *north*
nos: nos enfants *our*
children
notre: notre maison
our house
nouer *to tie*
nourriture (f) *food*
nous *we;* **nous deux**
both of us; **nous sommes**
we are; **c'est à nous** *it's*
ours; **c'est nous** *it's us;*
c'est pour nous *it's for us*
nouveau, (fem) nouvelle
new; **de nouveau** *again*
nouvelles (f pl) *news*
novembre *November*
nudiste (m) *nudist*
nuit (f) *night*
nulle part *nowhere*

numéro (m) *number*
(figure)

O

objectif (m) *lens* (camera)
objets trouvés (m pl)
lost property
obturateur *shutter*
(camera)
occupé *busy* (occupied)
octobre *October*
odeur (f) *smell*
œil (m) *eye*
œuf (m) *egg*
oignon (m) *onion*
oiseau (m) *bird*
olive (f) *olive*
omelette (f) *omelet*
oncle (m) *uncle*
ondulé *wavy* (hair)
ongle (m) *nail* (finger)
onze *eleven*
opérateur (m)
operator (phone)
opération (f) *operation*
opticien (m) *optician*
or (m) *gold*
orage (m) *thunderstorm*
orange (f) *orange* (fruit, color)
orchestre (m) *orchestra*
ordinateur (m) *computer;*
ordinateur portable (m)
laptop
ordonnance (f) *prescription*
ordre du jour (m) *agenda*
ordures (f pl) *litter;*
garbage
oreille (f) *ear*
oreiller (m) *pillow*
orgue (m) *organ* (music)
os (m) *bone*
ou *or*
où? *where?*
oublier *to forget*
ouest *west*
oui *yes*
ouvert (adj) *open*
ouvre-boîte (m) *can*
opener
ouvrir *to open*

P

page (f) *page*
paiement (m) *payment*
pain (m) *bread;*
pain grillé (m) *toast*
paire (f) *pair*
palais (m) *palace*
pâle *pale*

palmes (f pl) *flippers*
panier (m) *basket*
panne (f) *breakdown* (car);
je suis tombé
en panne *My car*
has broken down
pansement (m) *plaster*
pantalon (m) *pants*
pantoufles (f pl)
slippers
papa *dad*
papier (m) *paper;*
papier à lettres *writing*
paper; **papier cadeau**
gift wrap; **papier**
d'emballage *wrapping*
paper; **papier filtre** *filter*
paper; **papier hygiénique**
toilet paper
paquet (m) *package, packet*
par: *par avion air mail;*
par chemin de fer *by rail;*
par exemple *for example;*
par nuit *per night*
parapluie (m) *umbrella*
parasol (m) *sunshade*
parce que *because*
parcours de golf (m) *golf*
course
pardon!, pardon?
excuse me!; sorry! (apology);
pardon?
pare-brise (m) *windscreen*
pare-chocs (m)
bumper
parents (m pl)
parents
paresseux *lazy*
parfait *perfect*
parfum (m) *perfume*
parking (m) *parking lot*
parler *to speak, talk;* **parlez-**
vous ...? *do*
you speak ...?; ...
je ne parle pas ... *I don't*
speak
paroi (f) *wall* (inside)
parterre de fleurs (m)
flowerbed
parti (m) *party* (political)
particulièrement
especially
partout *everywhere*
pas *not;* **pas beaucoup** *not*
many; **pas encore** *not yet;*
il n'est pas ... *he's not ...*
passage (m) *driveway*
passager (m) *passenger*
passeport (m) *passport;*
passeport d'animaux (m)
pet passport

passe-temps (m) *hobby*
pastilles pour la gorge (f pl) *throat pastilles*
pâtes (f pl) *pasta*
patinoire (f) *ice rink*
patins à glace (m pl) *ice skates*
pâtisserie (f) *bakery, pastry shop*
pauvre *poor (not rich)*
payer *to pay*
pays (m) *country (state)*; **pays de Galles** (m) *Wales*
pêche (f) *peach; fishing:* **aller à la pêche** *to go fishing*
peigne (m) *comb*
peigner *to comb*
peinture (f) *paint; painting*
pelle (f) *spade (shovel)*
pellicule couleur (f) *color film*
pelouse (f) *lawn*
pendant *during*
pendule (f) *clock*
penser *to think*
pension complète (f) *full board*
père (m) *father*
perle (f) *pearl*
permanente (f) *perm*
permis (m) *license*; **permis de conduire** (m) *driver's license*
personne *nobody*
petit *small*
petit ami (m) *boyfriend*
petit déjeuner (m) *breakfast*
petite amie (f) *girlfriend*
petite-fille (f) *granddaughter*
petit-fils (m) *grandson*
petits pois (m pl) *peas*
pétrole (m) *paraffin*
peut-être *maybe; perhaps*
phares (m pl) *headlights*
pharmacie (f) *pharmacy*
photo (f) *photograph*
photographe (m/f) *photographer*
photographier *to photograph*
piano (m) *piano*
pickpocket (m) *pickpocket*
pièce (f) *coin; play (theatre)*
pièces de rechange (f pl) *spare parts*
pied (m) *foot*
piéton (m) *pedestrian*
pile (f) *battery (flashlight)*
pilote (m) *pilot*
pince (f): **pince à**

épiler *tweezers;* **pince à linge** *peg;* **pince à ongles** *nail clippers*
pinceau (m) *paintbrush*
pipe (f) *pipe (for smoking)*
pique *spades (cards)*
pique-nique (m) *picnic*
piquer *to bite (snake), sting (insect)*
piquet de tente (m) *tent peg*
piqûre (f) *bite (snake); sting (insect); injection*
pire *worse, worst*
piscine (f) *swimming pool*
piste (f) *runway; ski slope;* **piste pour débutants** *beginners' slope*
pistolet (m) *pistol*
piston (m) *piston*
pizza (f) *pizza*
placard (m) *cabinet*
place (f) *room (space); seat; square (in town)*
plafond (m) *ceiling*
plage (f) *beach*
plaisanterie (f) *joke*
plan (m) *town map*
plancher (m) *floor (ground)*
plan de travail (m) *countertop*
plancher (m) *floor (ground)*
plante (f) *plant*
plaque d'immatriculation (f) *license plate*
plastique (m) *plastic*
plat *flat (level)*
plateau (m) *tray*
plats (m pl) *main courses;* **plats préparés** (m pl) *prepared meals*
pleurer *to cry (weep)*
plombage (m) *filling (in tooth)*
plombier (m) *plumber*
plongeoir (m) *diving board*
plonger *to dive*
pluie (f) *rain*
plus *more:* **plus de** *more than;* **plus tard** *later;* **plus ou moins** *more or less*
plusieurs *several*
plutôt *quite*
pneu (m) *tire;* **pneu crevé** (m) *flat tire*
poche (f) *pocket*
poêle (f) *frying pan*
poignée (f) *handle (door)*
poignet (m) *wrist*
poire (f) *pear*

poireaux (m) *leek*
poison (m) *poison*
poisson (m) *fish*
poissonnerie (f) *fishmonger*
poitrine (f) *chest*
poivre (m) *pepper (and salt)*
poivron (m) *pepper (red/ green)*
police (f) *police*
policier (m) *police officer*
politique (f) *politics*
pommade (f) *ointment*
pomme (f) *apple*
pomme de terre (f) *potato*
pont (m) *bridge*
porc (m) *pork*
porcelaine (f) *china*
port (m) *harbor; port*
porte (f) *door (building);* **porte d'embarquement** (f) *gate (at airport)*
porte-bagages (m) *luggage rack*
portefeuille (m) *wallet*
porte-monnaie (m) *purse*
porteur (m) *porter*
portière (f) *car door*
porto (m) *port (drink)*
possible *possible;* **dès que possible** *as soon as possible*
poste (f) *mail; post office*
poster (m) *poster (inside); (verb) to post*
pot d'echappement (m) *exhaust (car)*
poubelle (f) *garbage can, trash can*
poudre (f) *powder*
poulet (m) *chicken*
poupée (f) *doll*
pour *for;* **pour moi** *for me;* **pour une semaine** *for a week*
pourboire (m) *tip (money)*
pourquoi? *why?*
pousser *to push*
poussette (f) *stroller*
pouvoir *to be able;* **je peux avoir ...?** *can I have ...?;* **vous pouvez ...?** *can you ...?*
préférer *to prefer*
premier *first;* **premier étage** (m) *first floor;* **première classe** *first class;* **premiers soins** (m pl) *first aid*
prendre *to take;* **prendre le train** *take the train;*

prendre un bain *take a bath*
prénom (m) *first name*
près de *near*; **près de la porte** *near the door*; **près de la fenêtre** *by the window*
préservatif (m) *condom*
presque *almost*
pressé: je suis pressé *I'm in a hurry*
pressing (m) *dry- cleaner*
prêt *ready*
prêtre (m) *priest*
prie: je vous en prie *you're welcome*
printemps (m) *spring (season)*
prise (f) *plug (electrical)*; **prise multiple** *adapter*
prise de sang (f) *blood test*
privé *private*
prix (m) *price*; **prix d'entrée** *admission charge*; **prix du billet** (m) *fare*
problème (m) *problem*
prochain *next*; **la semaine prochaine** *next week*
produit pour la vaisselle (m) *dishwashing liquid*
produits de beauté (m pl) *cosmetics*
produits entretien (m pl) *household products*
produits laitiers (m pl) *dairy products*
produits surgelés (m pl) *frozen foods*
professeur (m) *professor*; *teacher (secondary)*
profession (f) *profession*
profond *deep*
promener: aller se promener *to go for a walk*
propre (adj) *clean*
prudent *careful*; **soyez prudent!** *be careful!*
public (m) *public*
puce (f) *flea*
pull (m) *sweater*
punaise (f) *thumbtack*
pyjama (m) *pajamas*

Q

quai (m) *dock*; *platform*
qualité (f) *quality*
quand? *when?*
quarante *forty*

quart (m) *quarter*
quatorze *fourteen*
quatre *four*
quatre-vingt *eighty*
quatre-vingt-dix *ninety*
quatrième *fourth*
que *than*
quel âge avez-vous? *how old are you?*
quelle heure est-il? *what's the time?*
quelque chose *something*
quelque part *somewhere*
quelquefois *sometimes*
quelqu'un *somebody*
quelqu'un d'autre *someone else*
qu'est-ce que c'est? *what's that?*; *what is it?*
question (f) *question*
queue (f) *line*
qui? *who?*
quincaillerie (f) *hardware shop*
quinze *fifteen*; **quinze jours** *two weeks*

R

radiateur (m) *heater*; *radiator*
radio (f) *X-ray*; *radio*
radis (m) *radish*
rafraîchissements (m pl) *refreshments*
raie (f) *parting (in hair)*
raisin (m) *grape*; **raisin sec** (m) *raisin*
rallonge (f) *extension lead*
ramer *to row*
rames (f pl) *oars*
randonée (f) *hiking*
rapide *fast*; *quick*
rapport de police (m) *police report*
rare *rare (uncommon)*
raser: se raser *to shave*
rat (m) *rat*
râteau (m) *rake*
rayon (m) *aisle (supermarket)*
réception (f) *reception*
receptionniste (m/f) *receptionist*
réclamation de bagages (f) *baggage claim*
recommandé: en recommandé *registered mail*
record (m) *record (sports, etc.)*
reçu (m) *receipt*
réduction (f) *discount*
regarde: cela ne vous

regarde pas *it's none of your business*
regarder *to watch*
règle (f) *ruler*
rein (m) *kidney*
religion (f) *religion*
remercier *to thank*
remonte-pente (m) *ski lift*
remorque (f) *trailer*
rendez-vous (m) *appointment*
rendre *to return (give back)*; **rendre visite** *visit (person)*
repas (m) *meal*
repasser *to iron*
réponder (m) *answering machine*
reposer: se reposer *to rest (relax)*
reseignments (m pl) *directory (telephone)*
réservation (f) *reservation*
réserver *to book, reserve*
résistant *strong (material)*
respirer *to breathe*
ressort (m) *spring (mechanical)*
restaurant (m) *restaurant*
reste (m) *rest (remainder)*
retard (m) *delay*
retirer *to withdraw*
rétroviseur (m) *car mirror*
réunion (f) *meeting*
réveil (m) *alarm clock*
revenir *to return (come back)*
revue (f) *magazine*
rez-de-chaussée (m) *ground floor*
rhum (m) *rum*
rhume (m) *cold (illness)*; **rhume des foins** (m) *hay fever*
riche *rich*
rideau (m) *curtain*
rien *nothing*; **ça ne fait rien** *it doesn't matter*
rire *to laugh*
rivière (f) *river*
riz (m) *rice*
robe (f) *dress*
robinet (m) *tap (water)*
rocher (m) *rock (stone)*
rock (m) *rock (music)*
roman (m) *novel*
rond *round (circular)*
rondelle (f) *washer*
rond-point (m) *roundabout, rotary*
room service (m) *room service*
rose (f) *rose*; *pink (adj)*

rôti *roasted*
roue (f) *wheel*
rouge *red;* **rouge à lèvres** (m) *lipstick*
rougeur (f) *rash*
rouleaux (m pl) *curlers*
roux *red (of hair)*
rue (f) *street*
rugby (m) *rugby*
ruines (f pl) *ruins*
ruisseau (m) *stream (small river)*

S

sa: sa maison *his/her house*
sable (m) *sand*
sac (m) *bag;* **sac à dos** *backpack;* **sac à main** *handbag;* **sac de couchage** *sleeping bag;* **sac poubelle** *trash can liner*
saignant *rare (steak)*
salade (f) *lettuce; salad*
salle (f) *room;* **salle à manger** *dining room;* **salle d'attente** *waiting room;* **salle d'opérations** *operating room;* **salle de bains** *bathroom;* **salle de conférences** *conference room;* **salle de radiology** *X-ray departement;* **salle des urgences** *emergency room*
salon (m) *living room*
salut *hi*
samedi *Saturday*
sandales (f pl) *sandals*
sandwich (m) *sandwich*
sang (m) *blood*
sans *without;* **sans plomb** *unleaded*
santé! *cheers!*
s'arrêter *to stop*
sauce (f) *sauce*
saucisse (f) *sausage*
saumon (m) *salmon*
sauna (m) *sauna*
savoir *to know (fact);* **je ne sais pas** *I don't know*
savon (m) *soap*
science (f) *science*
seau (m) *bucket*
sec, (fem) sèche *dry*
sèche-cheveux (m) *hairdryer*
seconde (f) *second (of time)*
seconde: en seconde *second class*
secrétaire (m/f) *secretary*

secteur (m) *field (academic)*
sécurité: en sécurité *safe (not in danger)*
seize *sixteen*
sel (m) *salt*
semaine (f) *week*
séminaire (m) *seminar*
sentir *to smell*
séparé (adj) *separate*
séparer *to separate*
sept *seven*
septembre *September*
sérieux *serious*
seringue (f) *syringe*
séropositif(ve) *HIV- positive*
serveur (m) *waiter*
serveuse (f) *waitress*
service de pédiatrie (m) *children's ward*
serviette (f) *towel*
serviettes hygiéniques (f pl) *sanitary napkins*
ses: ses chaussures *his/her shoes*
seul *alone; single (one)*
seulement *only*
shampooing (m) *shampoo*
short (m) *shorts*
si *if; whether*
SIDA *AIDS*
siège pour bébé (m) *car seat (for a baby)*
siège social (m) *headquarters*
silencieux *quiet (person)*
s'il vous plaît *please*
simple *simple*
sirop (m) *syrup*
site web (m) *website*
six *six*
ski (m) *ski;* **faire du ski** *to go skiing*
skier *to ski*
slip (m) *underpants*
snack (m) *snack*
sœur (f) *sister*
soie (f) *silk*
soif: j'ai soif *I'm thirsty*
soir (m) *evening;* **ce soir** *tonight*
soirée (f) *party (get together)*
soit ... soit ... *either ... or ...*
soixante *sixty*
soixante-dix *seventy*
soldes (f pl) *sale (at reduced prices)*
soleil (m) *sun*
solution de trempage (f)

soaking solution (for contact lenses)
sommeil (m) *sleep*
somnifère (m) *sleeping pill*
son livre *his/her book*
sonnette (f) *bell (door)*
sortie (f) *exit*
sortie de secours (f) *emergency exit*
sortir *to leave*
soucoupe (f) *saucer*
soûl *drunk*
soupape (f) *valve*
soupe (f) *soup*
souper (m) *supper*
sourcil (m) *eyebrow*
sourd *deaf*
sourire (m) *smile;* *smile* (verb)
souris (f) *mouse*
sous ... *below ...; under ...*
sous-sol (m) *basement*
sous-vêtements (f pl) *underwear*
soutien-gorge (m) *bra*
souvenir (m) *souvenir; remember* (verb); **je m'en souviens** *I remember;* **je ne me souviens pas** *I don't remember*
souvent *often*
sport (m) *sport*
stade (m) *stadium*
stagiaire (m) *trainee*
station (f) *metro station*
station de ski (f) *ski resort*
station-service (f) *gas station*
statue (f) *statue*
steak (m) *steak*
store (m) *blind (window)*
stupide *stupid*
stylo (m) *pen;* **stylo-bille** (m) *ballpoint pen;* **stylo-plume** (m) *fountain pen*
sucette (f) *lollipop*
sucre (m) *sugar*
sucré *sweet (not sour)*
sud (m) *south*
suisse(sse) *Swiss*
Suisse: la Suisse *Switzerland*
supermarché (m) *supermarket*
supplément (m) *supplement*
suppositoire (m) *suppository*
sur ... *on ...*
sûr *sure*
survêtement (m) *jogging suit*

sweat-shirt (m) *sweatshirt*
sympathique *nice* (person)
synagogue (f) *synagogue*
syndicat d'initiative (m) *tourist office*

T

ta: ta maison *your house* (singular informal)
tabac (m) *tobacco; tobacconist*
table (f) *table*
tablette de chocolat (f) *bar of chocolate*
taille (f) *size*
taille-crayon (m) *pencil sharpener*
talc (m) *talcum powder*
talon (m) *heel*
tampon (m) *tampon*
tante (f) *aunt*
tapis (m) *carpet;* **tapis de sol** (m) *groundsheet*
tapisserie (f) *tapestry*
tard *late;* **bus est en retard** *the bus is late*
tasse (f) *cup; mug*
taux de change (m) *exchange rate*
taxi (m) *taxi*
télé cablée (f) *cable TV*
téléphérique (m) *cable car*
téléphone (m) *telephone;* **téléphone portable** (m) *cell phone*
téléphoner *to telephone* (verb)
télévision (f) *television*
témoin (m) *witness*
température (f) *temperature*
tempête (f) *storm;* **tempête de neige** (f) *blizzard*
temps (m) *weather; time;* **de temps en temps** *occasionally*
tennis (m) *tennis;* **les tennis** (m pl) *athletic shoes*
tente (f) *tent*
terminal (m) *terminal*
terrain de camping (m) *campground*
terrasse (f) *terrace*
terre (f) *land; soil*
tes: tes chaussures *your shoes* (singular informal; plural noun)
tête (f) *head*
thé (m) *tea*

théâtre (m) *theater*
ticket (m) *ticket* (underground, bus)
timbre (m) *stamp*
tire-bouchon (m) *corkscrew*
tirer *to pull*
tiroir (m) *drawer*
tissu (m) *material*
toboggan (m) *toboggan*
toi: c'est à toi *it's yours*
toilettes (f pl) *restrooms*
toit (m) *roof*
tomate (f) *tomato*
ton: ton livre *your book* (singular informal)
tondeuse à gazon (f) *lawnmower*
tongs (f pl) *flip-flops*
tonic (m) *tonic*
torchon (m) *dish cloth*
tôt *early*
toucher *to feel, touch*
toujours *always*
tour (f) *tower*
tourism (m) *sightseeing*
touriste (m/f) *tourist*
tourne-disque (m) *record player*
tournevis (m) *screwdriver*
tous les deux *both of them*
tousser *to cough*
tout *all; everything;* **tout droit** *straight ahead;* **tout le monde** *everyone;* **tout seul** *all alone*
toux (f) *cough*
tracteur (m) *tractor*
tradition (f) *tradition*
traducteur (m) *translator*
traduire *to translate*
train (m) *train*
tranquille *quiet* (street, etc.)
transpiration (f) *sweat*
transpirer *to sweat*
travail (m) *job; work*
travailler *to work*
traverser *to cross*
trèfle *clubs* (cards)
treize *thirteen*
trente *thirty*
très *very*
tricoter *knit*
triste *sad*
trois *three*
troisième *third*
trop *too* (excessively)
trottoir (m) *sidewalk*
tu *you* (singular informal); **tu es** *you are*

tunnel (m) *tunnel;* **le tunnel sous La Manche** *Channel Tunnel*
tuyau (m) *pipe* (for water)

U

un/une *a; one;* **un/une autre** *another* (different)
université (f) *university*
urgence (f) *emergency*
urgent *urgent*
utensiles de cuisine (f pl) *cooking utensils*
utile *useful*
utiliser *to use*

V

vacances (m pl) *vacation*
vaccination (f) *vaccination*
vague (f) *wave;* *faint* (adj)
valise (f) *case*
valise (f) *suitcase*
vallée (f) *valley*
vanille (f) *vanilla*
vapeur: à la vapeur *steamed*
vase (m) *vase*
veau (m) *veal*
végétarien (adj) *vegetarian*
véhicule (m) *vehicle*
vélo (m) *bicycle;* **vélo tout terrain** (m) *mountain bike*
vendre *to sell*
vendredi *Friday*
venir *to come;* **je viens de ...** *I come from ...*
vent (m) *wind*
vente (f) *sale* (transaction)
ventilateur (m) *fan* (ventilator)
vernis à ongles (m) *nail polish*
verre (m) *glass*
verres de contact (f pl) *contact lenses*
verrou (m) *bolt* (on door)
verrouiller *to bolt*
vert *green*
veste (f) *jacket*
vêtements (m pl) *clothes*
vétérinaire (m) *veterinarian*

viande (f) *meat*
vide *empty*
vidéo (f) *video* (film/tape)
vie (f) *life*
vieux, (fem) **vieille** *old*
villa (f) *villa*
village (m) *village*
ville (f) *city; town*
vin (m) *wine*
vinaigre (m) *vinegar*
vingt *twenty*
violet *purple*
violon (m) *violin*
vis (f) *screw*
visage (m) *face*
viseur (m) *viewfinder*
visite (f) *tour; visit*
visiter *to visit* (place)
visiteur (m) *visitor*
vitesse (f) *gear* (car); *speed*
vodka (f) *vodka*
voile (f) *sailing*

voilier (m) *sailboat*
voir *to see;*
je vois *I see;*
je ne vois rien *I can't see anything*
voiture (f) *car; train car*
voix(f) *voice*
vol (m) *flight*
volaille (f) *poultry*
volant (m) *steering wheel*
voler *to fly; steal;* **on a volé** *it's been stolen*
volet (m) *shutter* (window)
voleur (m) *thief*
vomir *to be sick* (vomit)
vos: vos chaussures *your shoes* (singular formal; plural; plural noun)
votre: votre maison *your house* (singular formal; plural; singular noun)

vouloir *to want;*
je veux *I want;*
vous voulez? *do you want?*
vous *you* (singular formal; plural); **vous êtes** *you are*
voyage (m) **trip,** *journey*
vrai *true*
vue (f) *view*

W, Y, Z

wagon-lit (m) *sleeper car* (train)
wagon-restaurant (m) *restaurant car* (train)
whisky (m) *whiskey*
yaourt (m) *yogurt*
yeux (m pl) *eyes*
zoo (m) *zoo*

Acknowledgments

The publisher would like to thank the following for their help in the preparation of this book: Anne-Marie Miller for the organization of location photography in France; Hôtel-Restaurant, "Le Rabelais", Fontenay le Comte; Gare Routière de Fontenay le Comte; Pharmacie Parot, Nieul Sur L'Autise; Garage Gouband, Oulmes; Musée de l'Abbaye de Nieul Sur L'Autise (Cabinet Tetrac, Nantes); Boulangerie des familles, Coulon; Fromagerie, rue St Marthe, Niort; Fruits et Primeurs Benoit, Halles de Niort; Gare SNCF de Niort; Magnet Showroom, Enfield, MyHotel, London; Kathy Gammon; Juliette Meeus, and Harry.

Language content for Dorling Kindersley by **G-and-W publishing**
Managed by **Jane Wightwick**
Editing and additional input: **Pamela Wightwick, Christine Arthur, Leila Gaafar**

Additional design assistance: **Phil Gamble, Lee Riches, Fehmi Cömert, Sally Geeve**
Additional editorial assistance: **Kajal Mistry, Paul Docherty, Lynn Bresler**
Picture research: **Louise Thomas**

Picture credits

Key: t=top; b=bottom; l=left; r=right; c=centre; A=above; B=below

p2 **Alamy:** *Ian Dagnall;* p3 **DK Images:** *Peter Wilson:* p4/5 **Alamy:** *f1 Online tl; images-of-france tr;* **Alamy:** *Andy Marshall bl;* **DK Images:** *br; Neil Lukas tcr;* p6/7 **Laura Knox:** *cl;* p10/12 **Alamy:** *BananaStock cAr; RubberBall cBl;* **Ingram Image Library:** *bl;* p12/13 **Alamy:** *John Foxx cAr; RubberBall br;* **DK Images:** *cl; Steve Shott cBr;* **Ingram Image Library:** *tr, cr;* p14/15 **Alamy:** *images-of-france tcr;* **Dreamstime.com:** *Slobodan Mračina (cr);* **Ingram Image Library:** *cAl, cl, cBl, cAr, cBr, bcr;* p16/17 **Alamy:** *RubberBall bcr;* **Ingram Image Library:** *tr;* p18/19 **DK Images:** *David Murray tr; Ian O'Leary clB;* p22/23 **DK Images:** *cl, Andy Crawford cAr; Susanna Price br; Magnus Rew tcrB;* **Ingram Image Library:** *bcl, tcr;* p24/25 **DK Images:** *clA, Dave King tcr;* p26/27 **Ingram Image Library:** *cl;* p28/29 **DK Images:** *Andy Crawford cr; Dave King cr; Matthew Ward bclA;* **Ingram Image Library:** *bcrA, bcr;* p30/31 **Alamy:** *Comstock Images bcl;* **DK Images:** *cl, bclA;* 34/35 **Dreamstime.com:** *Slobodan Mračina (cl);* **iStockphoto.com:** *nicolas_ (tcr);* p36/37 **DK Images:** *bcl, bcr; Magnus Rew cl;* **Dreamstime. com:** *Slobodan Mračina (cla);* **Ingram Image Library:** *bl;* **iStockphoto.com:** *nicolas_ (cr);* p38/39 **Alamy:** *Imageshop / Zefa Visual Media cl;* p40/41 **Alamy:** *images-of-france bl;* **Alamy:** *Justin Kase cAr;* **DK Images:** *cl, bcr;* p42/43 **Alamy:** *Artografika Bildagentur cr;* **Alamy:** *Image Source tcr, cAr; Andy Marshall cAAr;* p44/45 **Courtesy of Renault:** *c;* p46/47 **Alamy:** *Artografika Bildagentur cr; images-of-france cl;* **Alamy:** *Imageshop / Zefa Visual Media br;* **DK Images:** *bcl;* **Ingram Image Library:** *trlB;* **Courtesy of Renault:** *tcr;* p48/49 **Alamy:** *Agence Images tcr; Ian Dagnell c; PCL bcr; Peter Titmuss cr;* **DK Images:** *bcl;* p50/51 **Alamy:** *Robert Harding Picture Library c;* p52/53 **Alamy:** *imagebroker tcr;* **Alamy:** *Image Farm Inc cAr; Photov.com / Hisham Ibrahim tcrB;* **DK Images:** *cl;* p54/55 **Alamy:** *Frank Herholdt bcl; Jackson Smith cBl;* **Alamy:** *BananaStock c; John Foxx c; Image Source cAr; ThinkStock tcr;* **DK Images:** *Andy Crawford bclA;* p56/57 **Alamy:** *Agence Images clA; Ian Dagnell cl; PCL tl; Peter Titmuss cAl;* **DK Images:** *clAA; Courtesy of Renault:** *bc;* p58/59 **Alamy:** *Michael Juno tcr;* **Alamy:** *Brand X Pictures cBl, cBBl; Image Source cAAl;* **DK Images:** *cAl;* p60/61 **123RF.com:** *shutswis (clb);* **Alamy:** *Robert Harding Picture Library bcr;* **Alamy:** *Image Source cAr;* **DK Images:** *Steve Gorton bl, tcrB; Pia Tryde cAAr;* **Ingram Image Library:** *cr;* p62/63 **DK Images:** *Stephen Whitehorn c;* p64/65 **Alamy:** *Arcaid bcrA;* **Alamy:** *GKPhotography cBr; Goodshoot cAAr; imagebroker c; Justin Kase tcrB;* **DK Images:** *Steve Tanner cAr;* **Ingram Image Library:** *tcr;* p66/67 **Alamy:** *Arcaid tl;* **Alamy:** *Image Source cAr;* **DK Images:** *tr; Stephen Whitehorn bl;* **Ingram Image Library:** *br;* p68/69 **Alamy:** *Balearic Pictures cr; f1 Online cBl; Doug Houghton cl; Indiapicture clB;* **Alamy:** *images-of-france cBr; Justin Kase bl;* **DK Images:** *Peter Wilson cAl;* p72/73 **Alamy:** *imagebroker tcrB; Image Source cAr; Comstock Images tcr;* **Avery Weight-Tronix:** *bl;* p74/75 **Alamy:** *Doug Norman bl;* **Ingram Image Library:** *c;* p76/77 **Alamy:** *Balearic Pictures cBl; f1 Online clB; Indiapicture bl;* **DK Images:** *Peter Wilson bcl;* p80/81 **Getty:** *Taxi / Rob Melnychuk bc;* **Ingram Image Library:** *cAr;* **Xerox UK Ltd:** *tcr;* p82/83 **Alamy:** *wildphotos.com tcr;* **Alamy:** *FogStock cAAl; Momentum Creative Group cAl; Shoosh / Up the Res cBl;* **Ingram Image Library:** *c;* p84/85 **Alamy:** *Brand X Pictures cr; f1 Online c;* **Alamy:** *BananaStock bl; SuperStock tr;* **Ingram Image Library:** *crB;* p86/87 **Getty:** *Taxi / Rob Melnychuk bc;* p90/91 **Alamy:** *Brand X Pictures tcr;* **DK Images:** *cl; David Jordan cAr; Stephen Oliver cr;* **Ingram Image Library:** *cBr;* p82/93 **Alamy:** *Pixland cl;* **DK Images:** *cl; Guy Ryecart cr;* p94/95 **Alamy:** *David Kamm cl; Phototake Inc bcl;* **Alamy:** *Comstock Images cr; ImageState Royalty Free bcr;* **DK Images:** *Stephen Oliver cr;* p96/97 **Alamy:** *Pixland bcr;* **DK Images:** *tl;* **Ingram Image Library:** *tcr; bcrA;* p114/115 **Alamy:** *FogStock tcr; David R Frazier Photolibrary, Inc cBr;* **Alamy:** *Image Source cAr; Index Stock cAl;* **DK Images:** *Max Alexander cr;* p116/117 **Alamy:** *The Garden Picture Library cAl;* p118/119 **DK Images:** *Steve Gorton tcr;* **GettyNews:** *Giuseppe Cacace c;* p120/121 **Alamy:** *ImageState / Pictor International cl;* **Alamy:** *Sarkis Images tcr;* **DK Images:** *cBl, bcl; Kevin Mallett br;* p122/123 **Alamy:** *BananaStock cA;* **Ingram Image Library:** *cl;* p124/125 **Alamy:** *ImageState / Pictor International bclA;* **DK Images:** *cBl, bcl; Paul Bricknell tc(5); Geoff Dann tc(3); Max Gibbs tc(1); Frank Greenaway tc(2); Dave King tc(4); Kevin Mallett bl; Tracy Morgan tc(6);* p126/127 **Alamy:** *imagebroker clB;* **Alamy:** *© Hisham Ibrahim / Photov.com blA; Image Farm Inc bl;* p128 **DK Images:** *Neil Mersh.*

All other images **Mike Good.**